Rethinking
Language Arts

CRITICAL EDUCATION PRACTICE
VOLUME 9
GARLAND REFERENCE LIBRARY OF SOCIAL SCIENCE
VOLUME 1014

CRITICAL EDUCATION PRACTICE

SHIRLEY R. STEINBERG AND JOE L. KINCHELOE, *SERIES EDITORS*

Rethinking Language Arts
Passion and Practice

Nina Zaragoza

Garland Publishing, Inc.
New York and London
1997

Library of Congress Cataloging-in-Publication Data

Zaragoza, Nina.
    Rethinking language arts : passion and practice / by Nina Zaragoza.
        p.   cm. — (Critical education practice ; v. 9. Garland reference
library of social science ; v. 1014)
    Includes bibliographical references and index.
    ISBN 0-8153-1958-4 (alk. paper). — ISBN 0-8153-2322-0 (pbk. : alk.
paper)
    1. Language arts—United States.   2. Critical thinking—Study and teach-
ing—United States.   3.Critical pedagogy—United States.   4. Teachers—
Training of—United States—Philosophy.   I. Title. II. Series: Garland reference library of social science ; v. 1014. III. Series: Garland reference library
of social science. Critical education practice ; vol. 9.
LB1575.8.Z37   1997
372.6—dc20   96–34470
                                                        CIP

Cover photograph by Tony Donovan, The Ivoryton Studio.
Paperback cover design by Robert Vankeirsbilck.

Printed on acid-free, 250-year-life paper
Manufactured in the United States of America

I dedicate this book to all the children God has placed in my life, especially my sons Christian, Michael and Derek, and my Godchildren Daniel and Christine. May they hold fast to their dreams and to each other.

SERIES EDITOR'S PREFACE

Shirley R. Steinberg

Five years ago I was challenged to write a chapter entitled, "Teachers Under Suspicion," answering the question, "Are teachers as good as they used to be?" (Steinberg, 1992, 1995) I searched deeply into my own educational history to find a teacher who exemplified my contention that yes, teachers are as good, are better, than the mythological, Rockwellian vignettes that William Bennett and Rush Limbaugh contend were lost in the satanic sixties. As I reread my own schooling, I remembered a teacher who "changed my life." When I would write and speak to preservice teachers, I would often recall stories about Mrs. Gatsinaris, "Mrs. G."—a *good* teacher. Two years ago I visited a third grade classroom in Miami, Florida—I sat enchanted, enthralled, excited as I watched Nina Zaragoza work with thirty children in a democratic, creative and loving school environment.

I have never seen such complete engagement between students and teacher. These young girls and boys, all of whom were speaking English as a second language, were intimately familiar and comfortable with the possibilities, nuances of speaking, reading, and writing. To call Nina's class a "writer's workshop" seems, somehow, essentialized. There isn't one phrase or trendy word to label or categorize how she teaches. I can say, however, that Nina Zaragoza teaches within a democratic classroom, a room where children and adults feel secure and equal—a room, where, (as Nina recounts) students *really* don't know *where* the teacher's desk is. How often do we enter classrooms and encounter that desk, that central figure that marks the territory that Ms. or Mr. _____occupies? When Nina teaches, she learns, she works, she writes—sometimes the only distinguishable feature about Nina is that she is somewhat taller than her students.

Nina is a full-time professor at a university. Along with her duties of attending meetings, putting up with the inadequacies of a college of education and teaching her courses, she voluntarily works every day within an elementary classroom. Naturally, there is no funding to support Nina's teaching and research—however, the work that Nina does within the Dade County Public Schools in collaboration with teachers is complete, serious and revolutionary. Nina attends school each morning with her cooperating teacher companion; she engages the class as the co-teacher, then leaves at lunch time to join her "regular" job at Florida International University. Nina's students are companions within her lessons and are thrilled to gain the skills and abilities she shares with them. I remember a special morning when thirty Cuban-American children jumped up next to their desks to recite Langston Hughes to the "visitor." At that point, life hadn't been no "crystal stair" for many of these children, and the poem was a cross-cultural moment in a collective consciousness of childhood and living life in the real world. As these girls and boys eloquently recalled Hughes' words, I felt chills and wonderment at the utter joy each of them was experiencing as they *gave* me this poem as a welcome gift.

The best way to understand the phrase "good teacher" is to see one in action. This book is an opportunity for many people to have that experience. Nina is a transformative, energetic author who presents herself, her scholarship and her children to you in the form of personal letters. This book is the future of critical pedagogy—a theoretically informed, yet accessible view of teaching in the lived world of the classroom. Please enjoy it.

CONTENTS

RETHINKING
LANGUAGE ARTS

LETTER #1
INTRODUCTION

Dear Students,

The separation of philosophy and classroom methods increasingly concerns educators who believe good teaching includes a strong, philosophical foundation. Those who study to become teachers often find themselves denied the opportunity to reflect on the strong connections between philosophy and classroom practice. In fact, when I begin my methods courses with a few sessions of "philosophical discussions," I frequently hear the question, "When will we get to what we're suppose to do in the classroom?"

But when we separate philosophy from classroom practice lock-step, isolated, ungrounded instruction becomes a real danger. When we "send out" teachers who only have recipes to follow but really don't know why they follow them, we reduce our teachers to bureaucratic pawns obediently following directions. This text is not a cookbook. Instead it shows a respect for students and professors as reflective thinkers and encourages you to envision both how you will design a literacy program in the classroom and why you will design it that way.

This methods text is grounded in critical theory and works toward lessening the familiar plea "Tell me what to do" and broadening your views of yourselves as educators. The problem with "the language of critique" (Giroux, 1988), however, is that most members of our educational community have little experience with it. It can, I admit, intimidate the untrained ear (sometimes even the trained ear) and while theorists in critical theory (Giroux, 1988; Goodman, 1992; Grumet, 1988a, b; and Kincheloe, 1993) discuss such vital issues related to teacher education as the teacher as decision maker, reflective thinker, political being and social change agent, the discussion includes only a limited number of participants. "When the linguistic structure and terminology of this scholarship prevent the vast majority of like-minded scholars (let alone classroom teachers) from having little more than the slightest notion of what is being said after several readings, then it becomes at best a form of self-indulgent expression . . . at worst a form of psychic oppression" (Goodman, 1992, p. 166).

This text, therefore, helps connect classroom practice to the language of critique and provides a clear vision of alternative classroom environments founded on critical theory. In fact, this text links practice and the language of critique and thus addresses the concern that "a language of critique that is not rooted in vision of actual practice can potentially slip into dogma" (Goodman, 1992, pp. 168-169). In fact, it goes beyond the language of critique toward a language of possibility (Giroux, 1988).

The idea for this type of methods text came from one of my undergraduate language arts students who observed me teach language arts in my third-grade classroom. She had just had Joe Kincheloe for a philosophy of education course and was familiar with critical theory. She came up to me and asked, "Do you know Joe Kincheloe?" I told her I hadn't met him yet, and she replied "You two should get together. You do in the classroom exactly what he talks about. I couldn't imagine how to do half the things he talked about in a real classroom but now I can really see that it works!"

Discussions on how critical theory can "work" in a real classroom must begin to include others in the field—undergraduates, graduates and classroom teachers. These people must start to reflect critically on decisions and become "transformative intellectuals." Indeed, it seems ironic that while critical theorists talk about multiple ways of knowing, their writings often deny entry into these important conversations to those who interact most directly with students—classroom teachers. This text opens one door and invites educators to engage in critical conversations that encourage them to reflect and continually recreate so as to transform their classrooms into just and caring communities.

This text begins the journey from "visionary rhetoric to classroom reality, from curriculum critique to pedagogical possibility" (Simon, 1988). You will see and hear instances of real education and critical practice grounded in critical theory through lived experiences of educators and students. This text honors the stories we all tell, retell, read and reread for the "the reading and rereading of our stories create a linguistic bridge between our private and public worlds, between what we know and what we teach to others" (Grumet, 1988b). And so this text is my story as a public school teacher, a university professor, a single mother of three boys, a woman. As I offer my story I ask that teacher and student interpret it, for "it is in this process of interpretation, a process shared by teacher and student, that pedagogy and research fuse" (Grumet, 1988b).

Talk to you soon,

Nina

Nina

LETTER #2
THE REFLECTIVE EDUCATOR:
RETHINKING THE TEACHER AS PRACTITIONER

"[It's] not the thing done, but the quality of mind that goes into the doing."
(John Dewey, 1933, p. 215).

Dear Students,

Hi! As a professor of education I sometimes joke that whatever courses I'm slated to teach, they all turn out to be philosophy of education courses anyway. While at some level I say this to be amusing, at another level I am serious. How could any course in education fail in some way to be connected to philosophy? While the connection between philosophy and practice seems so evident and natural to me as I reflect on traditional teacher "training," I realize that my view is far from typical. Too often the faculty sees pre-service teachers as students who need to be taught the appropriate skills or recipes before they can be permitted into "classroom practice." This view is, of course, tied to a certain philosophical bent that sees learners as empty vessels to be filled, a view that sees teachers as needing to be "trained." This perception denies the real stories and knowledge of each student. I continually challenge the underlying assumptions with questions that revolve around personal stories and philosophy. When I examine and reflect upon these stories, I treat teachers as reflective thinkers instead of mere practitioners.

We need to critically examine the classroom teacher's role in whatever education course we become involved. We need to speak of the vision we have for ourselves as teachers. Indeed, each one of us must reflect upon who we envision ourselves to be: one who maintains the status quo or one involved in societal transformation.

I became a teacher because I envision myself as a social change agent in the elementary school. My choice of becoming a teacher is, in fact, a political statement in itself since I believe that schools mirror society and can, in turn, transform society. I believe that when we change education we do begin to transform society. I see myself as a powerful professional capable of reflecting on schooling and society and implementing effective curricula within the context of my classroom.

Unfortunately, traditional teacher "training" programs (I put this word within quotation marks because it implies that we can train people the way we train animals) promote an apolitical, aphilosophical, powerless and unreflective teacher profile. Various conceptions suggest what we need to concentrate on as we educate new teachers. Some consider it our job to train teachers. This approach assumes there is a certain body of knowledge that all teachers must possess, and its possession guarantees that the teacher is ready to teach. This approach would distribute recipes to follow so that all teaching remains standardized and essentially teacher-proof. This approach reinforces the competition so familiar within our educational system, encourages a fear of failure and a fear to be oneself.

Training proceeds through prepackaged curricula where one need only follow along. One has no need for powerful teachers and thinkers and no need for philosophy; one can just follow along. Indeed, this follow-along mentality nicely complements the idea that we can "train" teachers to "train" our students. This mentality permeates all aspects of our system—both schooling and society. One of the major questions you need to ask yourself is, "Do I want just to follow along?"

I decided I did not want to just follow along; I wanted to do the just, respectful, effective thing in all educational situations. How do I decide what is right and respectful? I make these decisions against a backdrop of strong philosophical and pedagogical beliefs. One of the first assignments I give is to ask my students to construct their own pedagogical philosophies. Many realize that they have never really thought about this before and some feel a bit intimidated by the process. To reassure them, I model some of my philosophical beliefs. Actually, I begin modeling them the minute students step into my classroom, which I usually set up in a circle of desks, like a seminar of equals:

> "Look how I have the room set up. What do you think this arrangement says about my philosophy of education?"
>
> "What do you think this type of physical classroom environment encourages?"
>
> "What type of interaction does this type of classroom foster?"
>
> "What does the physical design of this class tell you about what type of course this will be?"
>
> "What do you think I believe about students?"
>
> "What do you think I believe about teachers?"

Now I encourage you to reflect upon your beliefs. What do you believe about children? Do you see them as empty slates ready to be written upon, or as purposeful communicators wanting to tell their stories?

What do you believe your role as a teacher is? Do you believe that you are in the classroom to impart information to students who are "empty" vessels, or to help all your students tell their dynamic stories with power and conviction? Your answers to these questions will powerfully influence your classroom environment and all of your interactions. Indeed, what you believe about yourself and your students will influence what you do pedagogically. Put it this way: We all have a psychological philosophy and a pedagogical philosophy. What we believe about people psychologically should have a direct impact on our pedagogical philosophy—what we believe we need to do educationally in our classrooms. For example, if I believed that all students come to me with a valuable story to tell, my instructional environment would support this "story telling" by setting up opportunities for students to interact with me and their peers in discussion formats. If, on the other hand, I believed that children are blank slates or empty vessels in need of being "written upon" or "filled up," I would make sure to arrange my classroom so that I had daily opportunities to impart information to my students. If I believed that all children communicate purposefully and have the desire to be understood, I would ensure that my literacy environment contains a variety of opportunities for purposeful communication.

Do you think that you can pick and choose from various philosophical perspectives as the need arises? Some believe that they can and that they can decide what to do on the spot. While this approach has a superficial appeal because it appears you're meeting the needs of all your students, it usually runs into trouble along the way because your classroom techniques are not grounded in theory. Will you do "whatever works"? Think. Yelling works. If you want children to stop, yell in their faces and they will do what you want, at least for a while. Hitting children works too, at least for a while. So will you do what works or what is right, respectful and just? Please, take some time to think about this question deeply.

The importance of a personal philosophy of education can hardly be over-emphasized. What we believe and don't believe will have a major influence on all we do, say, don't do and don't say with our students. For example, my strong beliefs about learning and teaching permeate all I do and say as a third-grade teacher and as a university professor in a college of education. What do you strongly believe in? Think carefully about these issues. Start reflecting upon who you are, why you have chosen teaching as a profession, how you view this profession. I hope you begin to see yourself not as a bureaucrat or foot soldier ready just to follow orders but a critical reflective thinker who has decided to become a powerful member and transformer of society. Perhaps, this is the first time you've confronted these issues. But I encourage you to think hard about them even if the answers come slowly. They will come gradually as you reflect upon what you experience in and observe in classrooms and what you begin to envision for your own classroom.

I am a university professor who established a literacy project in a public school classroom so that I can teach all my language arts methods courses within a genuine classroom context. The classroom teacher and I teach both the third-graders and the language arts undergraduate students collaboratively. We address both the "hows" and the "whys" of instructional theory and practice. We address issues of power and different ways of knowing verbally and within the configuration of the project itself. We directly and constantly address the connection of philosophy and practice in the context of personal stories and reflection. We reflect upon the connections between the common text material we read, what we see in the classroom and our personal experiences to nurture the development of strong individual voices. This strengthening of personal voices will, in turn, fortify future educational communities.

One way we foster the personal voices of our undergraduates is by using personal reflective dialogue journals. The students write their personal reflections on classroom experiences and observations and receive responses from their professors or peers. When I read my students' journals, I find my thinking invariably stimulated by their insights, beliefs and feelings. For example, recently I read in a number of journals that the students were embarrassed when they participated in some of the third-grade activities.

To clarify a bit, my undergraduate students learn literacy within the literate community of the third-graders. That is, when third-grade children silently read, so do the undergraduate students; when third-graders write creatively, so do the undergraduates; when third-graders share their work, so do the undergraduates. In this way, a true community forms where all work is treated as worthwhile enough for everyone to do together. Undergraduates become actively involved in academic activities as well as activities that include good morning songs, goodbye songs and action songs. After one morning when all the undergraduates and third-graders sang and did hand and body motions to music, I read in a few of the students' personal journals that they felt "embarrassed" participating with the third-graders. This caused me to reflect upon what it really means when we say that we are embarrassed and how feeling this way relates to teacher education.

When we are embarrassed, we are probably worried about what others might think of us. This worry might mean we are afraid to show our true selves, afraid to be genuine, afraid to be who we are. Why are we afraid? Where does this kind of fear come from? The traditional system within which most of us have been educated forced us to compete so that only the strong survive and one person's success depends on another person's failure. Students in these situations are judged on whether they can perform as well as their peers. This type of judgement forces people to feel threatened by others and to fear that they will lose out on the limited resources. These types of classrooms deny students their personal strengths and gifts and see human potential through a narrow vision that idolizes one standard and denies the value of varied ways of knowing and being. In fact, these traditional classrooms force us to deny our true selves and become who we are expected to be.

I find the influence of this denial of personal strengths clearly illustrated in the university courses I teach. One of the first activities I ask my students to complete is to describe their strengths in writing. The majority of undergraduates admit feeling uncomfortable with this activity. In fact, many cannot complete it. When we are denied the opportunity to discover who we are and what makes us special, it can be difficult to be genuine and to be confident and unembarrassed.

As you already know, I understand my role as an educator at both the public school and university levels as an agent of social change. Accordingly, I advocate the establishment of a genuine classroom community where all members feel connected and responsible for each other. The development of such a community could begin to transform the competitive and threatening environments within which most of us have been forced to interact. The communities we create in the classrooms either maintain the status quo or transform our society into one where we all recognize and care for each other as valued members. When universities nurture students within communities that respect their expertise by allowing them full voice, our schools and society will be transformed. When these communities respect and validate the personal knowledge of both teachers and students within authentic, personal and passionate conversations, divisions caused by the fear of competition will begin to dissolve and our human connections will strengthen. When we establish cooperative and loving school communities, students learn that the resources they need, respect, safety and success are available for all.

Some believe, as I do, that our job is to educate individuals who can make professional decisions in a critical and reflective manner. This view would allow teachers to see themselves as growing and flexible intellectuals with valuable knowledge and experiences to share. It would also give them the time and structure for personal reflection, discussions and other opportunities so that they can get to know themselves, develop and strengthen their own personal voices and value who they are as individuals. Teacher education programs must encourage teachers to get to know themselves, who they are, and what their personal strengths are. We must establish welcoming environments so that teachers can accept and strengthen themselves. They will then feel secure enough to be genuine, be themselves, and be unembarrassed in their classroom community. Indeed, good teachers are obligated to be forthright, and to be who they are and who they are becoming for their students. The awakening of the "I" will enable us to join the "we" needed to form a caring human community.

Creating an Accepting Classroom at the University and Public School

1.   Personal dialogue journals both peers and educators have an opportunity to respond to.

2.   Flexible assignments that recognize students' expertise and strengths—for example, an open personal format for projects, choice of projects and reading materials, etc.

3.   Contextualizing course content within the individual experiences of students—for example, through the use of personal reflection papers on readings and discussions.

4.   Encouraging students to write in the first person so that their thoughts and beliefs become personal and strong.

5.   Group work that permits the group members and the projects and presentations to remain flexible so that all group members have the opportunity to be recognized for their strengths.

You've already heard a great deal about me and my beliefs. Now I want you to take the time to start connecting personally. Think about your answers to the following questions. Take your time. Don't worry if some of these questions leave you wondering, and don't worry if you lack all the answers at this point. As we continue to correspond I'm sure you will continue to develop some of these answers for yourself:

What do you believe about children?
What do you believe about how children learn?
What do you believe the purpose of schooling is?
What do you see as the child's role in the classroom?
What do you see as the teacher's role in the classroom?
Why do you teach?

Why do you read?

Why do you write?

Why are the answers to the questions above and other similar questions important in your development as an educator?

I bet some of you might be thinking, "Well, is she going to give us some of the answers?" Don't worry, you'll hear my answers throughout these letters. I want you to start thinking about your answers.

We have talked about the connection between our psychological and pedagogical beliefs and briefly about our view of teaching in society. Let's discuss this more. As I've already mentioned, I see myself as a social change agent. This means that I see teaching both as an educational act and a political act. As a matter of fact, education and politics cannot be separated. Teaching is a political statement since our educational system in various ways mirrors our society. What societal-political practices does our traditional way of education maintain? Think about it: What habits and behaviors do we reinforce (force children to do) that strengthen the status quo?

Think, as well, about the way we traditionally assess. Can all our children succeed? No, because we have set up a standard—the celebrated A—that only a few can attain. Let's translate this question to society. Are all people successful? No, some meet the standards of beauty, wealth and intelligence. They get A's. Some do not. They get F's. Indeed, because some of our students are far off the acceptable standard, they must leave the regular classroom for "special" classrooms. The citizens who meet our standards remain in the mainstream while those who haven't do not. We'll revisit this theme of separation constantly as I encourage you to see yourself as reflective, transformative educators who consciously participate in the educational process from psychological, political and pedagogical perspectives.

As reflective people, we do not just live our experiences, we also reflect upon them. This reflection gives meaning to these experiences and enables us to make future decisions. As I often tell my students, we can accept the myth that humans are "creatures of habit" or we can think about who we really are. We have the ability to choose. We can choose to go along because that's the way things are, or we can choose to exercise this uniquely human ability to reflect. John Dewey's observation noted in the beginning of this letter seems to fit right here. This quality of thought is crucial in all our educational decisions. Will you reflect or just do? Will you be a creature of habit or a reflective decision maker? I hope you have come to our field to lead—whether as a classroom teacher, school administrator or college professor. We desperately need educators who want to do more than just maintain a system that allows only a small number to have a voice. We need educators who will critically examine our system and who choose to reflect on past experiences and practices in order to encourage a just and respectful transformation. We desperately need visionaries in our schools who can look past the real world to new possibilities. Frankly, I'm a little impatient with the continuous litany of "But" statements I hear from many students—especially graduates already working in the field:

But that's reality.
But I have too many students in my class.
But I teach special ed.
But my students don't speak English.
But my students are too _____.
But they say I have to do _____.
But my administrator says _____.
But the parents won't understand.
But this is an inner-city school.
But these kids can't _____.
But there're only so many hours in a day.
But that's too idealistic.
But that's impossible.

These "But" statements demonstrate a hopeless paralysis. I suppose this is understandable and deserves continued discussion, but let's pair this discussion with reflection and action. We can endlessly blame our administrators, our children, their parents or the neighborhood and thus reinforce our feelings of hopelessness, or we can choose to act. We can decide to use up all our energy on blame, or devote it to examining ourselves and deciding on what we can do—what battles we are willing to fight and then begin fighting them. The people I want to join me in my field decide to be fully present in mind, spirit and body. They are willing to make difficult decisions about philosophy, practice and battles. Anyone off the street can say, "But it's impossible." I don't want anyone off the street in my profession. I want those who are will look beyond impossibilities and see possibilities. Will you do that?

Think about why you have decided to teach. Is it because it seems like a familiar and safe job? This is a common reason because all of us have been part of the educational system for at least twelve years. We know the rules, the expectations, the standard ways of interaction. Some might think, "Hey, how hard can it be, right? I've been in school all my life!" During my undergraduate program I had classmates who chose teaching because "When I get married and have a family I'll be home in time for my own children," or "I always liked school and besides what other job gives you a two month summer vacation?" or "Well, I'll teach so that I can bring in a second income for the family."

I wonder whether these attitudes are actually harming our profession and the students we teach. What do you think? I wonder if those who enter teaching because it is familiar have a hard time taking risks. If so, this type of person will probably find it easier to maintain the status quo and be uncomfortable with the risk-taking involved in transformative education. I worry about people whose main reason entering into education is the long summer vacation. Is this still happening? How many of our teachers consider education a stopgap job? For example, one of my graduate students recently shared this account:

> There is a teacher in my school who has just come into teaching and seems like he is a bit unsure. I offered him help with ideas and after a short time as he was trying out some of the stuff, he seemed to give up. He said to me "Oh, it really doesn't matter. This is just a temporary job until something better comes along."

Does anyone you know express similar attitudes? How does it make you feel?

The other day my graduate class, most of it full-time teachers in the public school system, and I were talking about some of the obstacles we encountered in the school system: isolation ("I don't even know the name of the teacher next door"), not enough time to share new ideas, the teachers who feel threatened by attempts to share, unconnected workshops, and so forth. As I encouraged them to go beyond these realities and think about how to transform them, one student suggested, "Well, instead of those workshops they should just put us into sharing groups. This is how we really learn about what others are doing and hear about what's really going on in their classrooms."

While I agree with this idea of discussion seminars, something struck me about the way this teacher worded her suggestion. Let's look at it: "They should just put us into. . . ." What type of teaching behavior does this statement illustrate? Who is the subject? Who is the object?

Think about it. This teacher has put herself and her profession in the position of object. She passively awaits the subject—"They"—to act upon her world and make it more bearable. Should we leave our lives up to others? While the system certainly places constraints on us, we might more effectively deal with some of them as active participants. So instead of saying, "They should put us into sharing groups," how about, "We need to form discussion groups so that we can share what we're doing in our classrooms." Notice the difference. In this last statement we the educators become the active agents and make the decision to do what we need to do, not wait for others to do it for us. These are the people I want in education: people who will become active participants in our educational community; who will not wait to be acted upon but will decide what is needed and then act on this decision. How do you see yourself as a teacher?

Traditional teacher training can make this question difficult for many entering the field. If you've become familiar with the view of education as a mechanistic-bureaucratic endeavor where you need only listen to directions and follow what the manuals say, you might find it difficult to see yourself as a strong and active decision maker. But, in fact, we are all decision makers because, consciously or not, we do decide what position we want to take—active or passive, subject or object. To become a critically conscious professional, we must continually work on developing our own personal voice. If you are going to be the subject of your life, you must know "I." Do you really know who you are? As I mentioned earlier, a strong self is crucial to the formation of a safe and caring community both within our individual classrooms and within our profession. We need strong and healthy professionals for our children and ourselves.

Educators enter classrooms to meet the needs of their students. While many of us also feel fulfilled with our choice of profession and so meet some personal needs, we are still there to go beyond our own needs to serve others. To serve others well, we must feel secure and safe with ourselves. As we've already discussed, when we value ourselves, we feel less threatened by others and can interact lovingly. I'm sure you realize that we educators have a powerful influence on our students. Think about your own school experiences. I'll bet your most powerful memories concern either extremely negative or positive events. I suspect some of the negativity we have encountered in school stems from teachers who felt insecure or threatened.

I'll never forget the time in fourth grade I asked Mrs. Scala a math question, a long-division question to be exact. I guess I asked one question too many because she bent down near me, her face beet red, her blue eyes wide under the wire-framed glasses, her steely gray curls quivering as she yelled at the top of her lungs, "I've explained this enough! If you don't understand it by now it's just too bad!" I can still hear her voice ringing in my ears, feel my face burning with shame and the spit from her mouth mixing with my tears.

This is the kind of person I want to keep out of our classrooms. This is the kind of person who feels threatened by questions and allows personal issues and struggles to block compassionate interaction. Have you ever experienced such a person? Do we have any right whatsoever to humiliate or degrade any student? We do not need people in the classroom trying to meet their own needs for power, control and validation. We need healthy, whole people who are psychologically secure. Perhaps you're thinking "Wow, I guess she expects us to be perfect." No, we don't have to be perfect. But we need to concentrate on personal growth so we can continue to strive to serve our students well. The healthier we are, the better able we are to promote a healthy community.

Part of your job, then, as a reflective practitioner is to reflect on your psychological needs. What issues might you need to begin resolving? Do you have a tendency to notice only your weaknesses? Are you a perfectionist? Are you sarcastic? Must you always be in control? How might these tendencies negatively influence your classroom interactions? Let's take one at a time and examine how these tendencies will negatively influence your classroom.

Deficit View

Many of us have a knack for pinpointing our problems. We can quickly draw up a list of things we can't do. I can't spell; I can't add; I'm a terrible writer! While some argue it's important for us to examine our weaknesses, a real danger lies in becoming obsessed with them. This obsession invites us to put obstacles in our own way. Of course, our competitive society encourages this deficit view because comparison is inherent in competition. We've had lots of practice comparing ourselves to others and now it almost comes naturally. Unfortunately, this view can easily invade our classrooms to set up barriers for those students who are not "the best."

But when we shift to a strength perspective—listing what we do best—we confront a number of conditioned objections. Many of us feel ourselves arrogant when we talk about what we do best. We've been taught to be humble and not to brag. These commendable behaviors, however, still permit us to be positive and honest with ourselves. We all have special gifts and talents we are meant to share with others. We need not flaunt them, but we do need to recognize them and use them for the larger community.

You will notice that this book continually and fully recognizes the strengths of all children. I see all children as gifted and experts in many areas. Moreover, they are all able and obligated to work in groups and use their gifts to help their peers grow academically and socially.

Perfectionism

Many of us tend to be perfectionists and some of us consider this characteristic a great strength. We repeat a task over and over again until we get it perfect. We stay up until three in the morning polishing a paper until it's just right. We make sure there is not one speck of dust on the furniture, especially when we expect company. But when we bring this characteristic into the classroom it can have devastating effects.

Think about it. When a teacher needs everything to be perfectly organized in the room, who do you think will be doing most of the decorating? Do you think that teacher will allow the children much say in the design? I don't think so. Perfectionists usually need to do it themselves. But when they do it themselves, they keep children from becoming full participants. Here is the message the perfectionist sends: "This is my room. Now, let's make sure we keep everything in place just the way it is now— my way."

This desire for perfection appears in academic work as well. In this classroom, the teacher generally has one standard or "perfect way" of proceeding and all other ways are less acceptable. So for example, unless your story has a fully developed beginning, middle and end it is not a story. Unless you read at a certain grade level, you are not reading acceptably. Indeed, the desire for academic perfection practically guarantees that only a few will measure up to the narrow and exclusive standards. I'll return to this issue as I continually challenge you to broaden your definitions and standards so that all children become successful participants in your classroom.

Sarcasm

Sarcasm cuts like a knife to the core of one's being. It is hurtful and has absolutely no place in our interactions with students. When I say this to my students, I generally hear such comments as "Oh, come on Nina, it's just a form of humor. I like to play around with my students." But is sarcasm really humor? It does makes people laugh but at whose expense? One person usually sits as the target of a sarcastic remark, and its purpose is to cut that person down by focusing on a vulnerable or weak area. In fact, one of the reasons sarcasm is so prevalent in our society today (turn on any sitcom) is its focus on the weaknesses of others. This focus reinforces our tendency to first notice the weaknesses in others and ourselves.

Sarcasm also offends me because it is a twisted, dishonest form of interaction. I tried to think of some examples of sarcastic classroom remarks but discovered that these examples would lose all usefulness in print because sarcasm requires both a context and a certain tone of voice. "Oh, beautiful" looks positive in print, but add a sarcastic tone of voice and then accuse a child of "scribbling" on his or her worksheet and you can almost feel the sting. That teacher did not think the child's work was beautiful at all but used the word to send the opposite message. This manipulation of message and feelings reveals one of the most degrading forms of power. If you have a tendency to use sarcasm, I urge you to examine your need to set up this type of interaction. I'm hoping that with continued reflection and work towards growth you will replace it with the power of loving encouragement and support in your classroom.

Power/Control

Associated closely with perfectionism we find the whole issue of power and control. We often need to exert power over someone when we feel out of control in other areas of our lives. When we feel like an object on which outside forces, act we feel out of control. We must manifest our natural need to feel empowered and in control somewhere. Thus, we arrange and organize. When we have the power to say that this is right and that is wrong, we feel powerful and in control. When we yell at a child, we feel powerful. In these situations we become the subjects acting upon the objects. I was the object Mrs. Scala acted upon. I was shamed and humiliated; she was the one with all the power.

The most dangerous teachers are those who lose control in their personal lives and use their classrooms to gain it back. If these people see teaching as safe and familiar—a situation they can control—they will, indeed, exert total control. We as reflective practitioners need to work continually on our self-growth to avoid using our students and classrooms as means for resolving these issues of power and control. We need to become the subjects—the major players—of our lives so we have no need to act upon someone else harmfully. One way to do this is to make conscious decisions that will enrich us and strengthen us individually. Think about some of the ways you can help yourself to grow—not just academically but in other ways as well.

Toward Continued Self-Growth

1. Read! Read! Read! (anything—books, magazines, even comics)
2. Write! Write! Write! (anything—lists, diaries, letters, even novels)
3. Learn something new outside of teaching like a musical instrument, a sport, a language, flower arranging, gardening, painting.
4. Exercise.
5. Take a trip. It doesn't have to be around the world. Visit your local park!
6. Pursue a long-lost dream.
7. Try group or individual therapy.
8. Join a discussion or outdoors group, a camping club, a film society.
9. Go to concerts, operas, art shows, museums.
10. Listen to music.
11. Sing a song.
12. Talk with a child, talk with a friend, talk with a stranger.
13. Play a board game.
14. Watch "Jeopardy."
15. Meditate, pray.
16. Rest.
17. Enjoy your life and enjoy who you are becoming.

Did any of you think teaching would be easy? I guess after this second letter you're beginning to wonder. I just finished rereading *The Unbearable Lightness of Being* by Milan Kundera, and it definitely speaks to our situation. Tomas, one of the main characters, is a doctor struggling with the issue of mission—of "weight." A variety of circumstances forces him into a change of occupation, and as a window-washer he begins to understand the state of blissful indifference one feels in a job that is light and carries no weight. Those of us who feel an internal call to teach can understand this feeling of mission. I challenge you to accept this weight if you feel called, for "the role of an educator who is pedagogically and critically radical is to avoid being indifferent, a characteristic of laissez-faire educators. The radical has to be an active presence in educational practice " (Freire and Macedo, 1987, p. 140).

I wish you passion and growth,

Nina

Nina

LETTER #3
TEACHING WITHIN COMMUNITY:
RETHINKING BLOCKED SCHEDULES

Good Morning Educators!

Most school districts schedule language arts in a two-hour continuous block. I've always wondered "So what are we doing the rest of the day when we communicate? (I hope we communicate!) Therefore, let me begin to explain to you concretely what happens in these two hours. A lot happens, and just thinking about it leaves me breathless.

As the children arrive at 8:20 I greet them and they greet me with "Good Morning!" They walk to their desks, take down the chairs which are on top of their desks so the custodians can sweep easily. They do not just take their own down but those around them. (Why? What am I reinforcing, modeling, encouraging, expecting here?) When all chairs are down, children begin to organize their desks, placing their homework, silent reading books and diaries at the corner of each desk. While awaiting the entire community's arrival, the children begin various activities—silently reading, making entries in their diaries, checking over their homework. When school-wide announcements begin, we come together as a class and listen. What do you think I do during these morning announcements? You're right, I listen too. I am a member of the community; therefore, I need to model and be involved in all the class activities, as well. Some mornings the announcements creep on at length and have absolutely nothing to do with the children. At these times, I let them continue writing in their diaries or silently reading.

After the announcements we can do a number of things, depending on how much time we have, what the children want, or what I want. Usually on Mondays, because we haven't been together for two days, we spend some time sharing. As I or a student take attendance the following interaction might happen:

Nina:	Good morning, Jessica. Do you want to tell us something?
Jessica:	Yes, I went to the beach yesterday and I saw a jellyfish.
Nina:	Oh, I've seen those, too! Has anyone else seen a jellyfish before? Has any one ever been stung by one? (Various students respond; either I acknowledge each or Jessica does.)
Nina:	(with the next attendance card) Good morning, Alex. Do you want to tell us something?

Conversation continues as I go through the attendance cards so that each child shares and receives a response. Notice that in this instance the question, "Do you want to tell us something?" allows all the children to choose if they want to share and what they want to share. Here, again, I promote the development of a strong, personal voice. Here, too, we continue building our ties as a community as we listen and respond to each other respectfully.

If we don't have as much time or want to get right into our reading and writing, I use a faster version of attendance:

> Nina: When I call your name tell us your most favorite word. George.
> George: Pizza.
>   (Usually everyone says "Yum" in unison, including me since
>   I love pizza.)
> Nina: Lourdes.
> Lourdes: Peace.

Most times when we use this format, I hand the attendance card to a child who decides on how the community should respond. To ensure that I keep choosing different children to do this, we follow the class list posted on the door. In this way, I relinquish control because the students know who will take attendance next. I never use taking attendance as a reward and we don't have "special helpers." In a critically conscious classroom everyone is responsible for the community's smooth operation. Here are some of the response ideas that my children have suggested:

> When I call your name tell us your:
>   -favorite book. Why?
>   -favorite author. Why?
>   -favorite sport. Why?
>   -favorite football player. Why?
>   -favorite movie. Why?
>   -favorite television show. Why?
>   -favorite poem. Why?
>   -what you're working on in writing.
>   -what book are you going to read next. Why?

Notice that after each contribution, the children make sure to hold their peers accountable for defending their opinions. Here we are early in the morning, children are reflecting critically upon all our responses!

Other mornings we might take attendance by singing a song that names every child:

> Hello, everybody how do you do? How do you do? How do you do?
> Hello everybody, how do you do? We love you today. If your name's
> Juan, stand up. If your name's Elena, stand up. If your name's Tasha,
> stand up. If your name's Richard, stand up. Hello everybody, how do you
> do?

The children usually clap the rhythm as we sing, and many move their bodies to the rhythm, too. Sometimes we change the "stand up" to other actions like "If your name is Tasha, shout 'Yes!','," stamp your feet, wave hello, and so forth.

If we don't begin with this kind of name song, I make sure to include some song right before or after attendance. One favorite is a Swahili song, "Jambo," which means "Hello."

> Jambo, Jambo, Jambo sana Jambo
> Hello, Hello, Hello everybody Hello
> Jambo, Jambo, Jambo watoto Jambo
> Hello, Hello, Hello children hello.

My own favorite song is a popular children's song "Say Hello" by Gregg and Steve (1985). It is an echo song (each line is repeated) that talks about friendship, love and community:

We also write our own songs like this one called "Good Morning":

> *Good Morning*
> Let's say good morning!
> Good morning!
> Is everybody ready to write and read
> And jump (children jump here) in the fun!

I wonder if any of you are thinking, "OK, Nina! Enough about good morning attendance. We get the picture! Let's get on with the schedule!" Okay, I hear you. But I have to say that taking attendance is a part of my literacy program.

Why do you suppose I consider such morning interactions are such an important part of a classroom that reflects a critical perspective?

Well, how many of us really say good morning to each other? Now, think about what happens in our schools. Who usually says good morning to whom? Have you ever walked down a school hallway in the morning as both teachers and children stream in? Have you noticed who says good morning to whom and who does not say good morning to whom? I have. I have seen adults pass children in the hall as if they were invisible. No "Good Morning," no eye contact, nothing. Yet three steps down the same hallway the same adult will wish a cheery "Good Morning!" to a fellow adult.

What a sad commentary on how adults feel about children. They are not worth even a courteous "Hello," or "Good Morning," or even a friendly nod of the head. What does this early discourtesy have to do with language arts instruction? Language arts teaches ways of expression. Ideally, it should allow or encourage children to express themselves as they truly are becoming. Language arts is ultimately a matter of respect for children's worth, for children's growth, for children's being. When I see a teacher who will not or cannot genuinely and naturally acknowledge a child's presence in the hallway, I wonder how willing he or she is to accord genuine respect during classroom instruction and interaction.

Homework

I always contextualized homework within the ongoing interactions in the classroom. In a classroom predicated on dialogue, there is no way to totally predict what homework will emerge. Since our literacy program is driven by the community experiences and reflection on these experiences through discussions I try to remain open and listen for meaningful work to do at home. Here is such an instance:

Nina: Let's think of something we can do for homework that's connected to our play about the four habitats. Any ideas?

Richard: We could read the script over and pick our favorite words.

Nina: Okay. Others?

Debbie: How about picking our spelling words from the script?

Elliott: I was thinking since the play is dedicated to Marjory Stoneman Douglas why don't we invite her?

Nina: Sounds good. So what could our homework be, then?

Sally: Write an invitation to Marjory Stoneman Douglas.

Nina: Okay. Why don't we do that for tonight. Also, anyone who would like to pick out their favorite words or some new spelling words you can do that, too. So raise your hand if you are going to do all three of those things? Raise your hand if you will only write the letter to Marjory Stoneman Douglas tonight? That's okay. As long as everyone at least writes the invitation. What I'll do is find her address so we can mail them to her tomorrow.

Note that I, consciously, kept from praising each idea because I did not want to promote one idea as having more value than another. I purposely allowed all responses before I responded. (We must always be conscious of our power and influence in the classroom and how we exert or don't exert it.) Notice, too, that while I made the final decision on the major homework assignment by providing the option to do all the suggested ideas, I negated none of them. I often allow even more choice:

Nina: Okay, since we've been talking about persuasive writing for a couple of weeks, let's do a homework connected to persuasive writing. Any ideas?

Maria: How about we write a commercial for our favorite book?

Elena: Or we can try and convince our parents about something?

Nina: What do you mean?

Robert: Like trying to convince them to buy us a tv or to let us go someplace.

Nina: Okay. Someone else?

Kamala: Maybe asking the principal something.

Nina: Like what?

Tania:	Like in our play—when Brian and Melissa invented the ice cream machine—we can ask the principal to get us an ice cream machine for the cafeteria.
Nina:	Wow! I like how you connected to our play! Another idea?
Billy:	We could try and convince someone to take us to Disney World.
Nina:	You all have some great ideas. Why don't you just decide on what you want to do for homework? As long as it's connected to persuasive writing. Do we all always have to do the same homework?
Pauline:	No.
Nina:	Why not?
Gene:	Because we all don't have to like the same things.
Nina:	That's right. And if you like your homework, do you think you'd do a better job at it?
Lauren:	Yes.
Nina:	Why?
Walter:	'Cause when we like it we will put our mind to it more.

Here the children become full participants in their learning. They are reflective decision makers taking the role seriously. I am a facilitator, of course, but they are facilitators as well.

Children always have what I call "standing homework," on-going assignments to be addressed consistently over time:

1. Study poetry (usually when we are working on a specific poem its name is placed here). For example, study "Dreams" by Langston Hughes, or think of movements for "Mother to Son" by Langston Hughes (1994).
2. Study spelling.
3. Continue personal reading.
4. Work on individual presentation.
5. _____ . (Emergent homework goes here.)

I can, of course, make certain adjustments depending on the current work at hand. For example, when we are putting a lot of our energy into our drama production "Study poetry" changes to "Study script" or "Think of problem and solution for drama production." We'll talk more about the need for relevant homework as our correspondence continues.

Silent Reading Books

The silent reading books my children have at the corner of their desks vary in levels, topics and numbers. They usually have either three to four different books. Some have as many as ten. For example, the whole "Goosebumps" or "Babysitters' Club" series. The enthusiasm that these books can engender is incredible:

Nina:	Wow, Eileen you really have a lot of books at the corner of your desk! Do you think you'll get to read them all today?
Eileen:	I hope so! I'm going to try to read each one of them at least a little.
Nina:	That's great. I can tell you really do like to read!

These silent reading books generally stay on the desk most of the time, and the children read them both during silent and team reading and at other moments throughout the day. When the teacher next door comes in and interrupts a class discussion, the children will read as they wait. Also, while I usually reserve one block of time for reading during the day we might decide to go into reading again to have a break from a strenuous activity or just for the sheer pleasure of reading again. We'll talk much more about this pacing when we discuss reading process in more detail later.

Diaries

The children take their personal diaries out of their desks and write in them after placing their silent reading books and their homework at the corner of their desks. Most of this writing takes place as the children enter the room, and they have usually finished before the general announcements begin. They all make entries in these diaries every day. I never guide their entries, and I never address spelling and writing skills in connection with the diaries. I respond only to the content, and my only requirement is that the entries appear each day. If the children want to make private entries, they fold the page to hide them. They usually write such orders such as "No Trespassing!" "Keep Out!" "Do Not Look!" and "Private." These requests are, of course, honored.

When children are writing in their diaries I either quietly circulate around the room and encourage them or write in my own diary. Again, think about the messages I send my students. By circulating around the room, I tell them they are important to me and their writing has value. Also, by writing in my own diary, I reinforce the importance of diary writing and my own place as a part of the community.

After the attendance activity the children are usually standing, so we go into another activity that requires standing:

Nina:	Since everyone is standing what should we do now?
Jessica:	Another song?
Nina:	Okay. Another idea?
Mike:	Poetry.
Nina:	Okay, let's do that since we just finished a song. Stage posture. (Students stand in stage posture which is feet together, body straight, hands down at their sides.)
Nina:	Good. Okay, Ann call out the poem you want us to practice. (I might have chosen Ann because she was the first one on the class list or she was next in line on the list to call out a poem.

I use the list like this to give all the children an equal chance at the activity.)

Ann: "Dreams" by Langston Hughes.

All: "Dreams" by Langston Hughes.

Hold fast to dreams,
For if dreams die,
Life is a broken-winged bird,
That cannot fly.
Hold fast to dreams,
For when dreams go,
Life is a barren field,
Frozen with snow.

Nina: Excellent! Beautiful expression and I like how everyone did the movements we made up yesterday. Give yourselves a hand. Now let's all get on line for P.E.

Notice, that going from one standing activity to another wastes virtually no transition time. Also, because most mornings my children go out for an hour of special class instruction, I plan a standing activity right before they need to get on line. We save transition time here as well. While I know this might seem like only seconds, put all these seconds together and you save whole minutes for purposeful work.

When my children return to the classroom from outside special classes—phys ed, music, art, computer, library—they are usually ready to calm down and begin to focus on the plans ahead. Therefore, quiet, solitary work does well, and here is when I often suggest that the children silently read the books already placed at the corners of their desks.

After silent reading we go into team reading where children discuss their silent reading material with a group of their classmates. The groups are flexible and the children usually choose their groups. I guide these discussions with specific questions or tasks (for example, "In your groups I want you to talk about the character traits of one character in your story"), or I leave the children to develop their own questions. I plan to discuss the details of silent reading and team reading in my sixth letter.

After silent and team reading, children usually go into the writers' workshop where they work through the stages of the writing process as they create pieces of personal narrative. Different children are in different stages of the process, so some talk about ideas for drafts, work on incomplete drafts, revise or edit, or publish edited drafts into homemade hard-covered books. They write these drafts either in a spiral-bound notebook or on loose sheets of paper in a folder. This writing is completely separate from diary entries because it is not private but meant for an audience.

As the children write, I help with individual editing, talking with children about their work or writing myself. Sometimes during writing workshop I bring all children together ("Let's all come together as a class, please") and discuss a certain skill within the context of a child's written work. Writers' workshop also includes time for sharing work as a full class. This usually takes place after the children have been writing individually for about twenty minutes. Three children sign up each day to share their work in front of the class. Part of this time also includes class responses to this work. Full class sharing usually takes about 15 or 20 minutes. Within this time, too, I might give a quick contextualized skills lesson. Writers' workshop and contextualized skills lessons will receive fuller treatment in subsequent letters.

Because during writing there is much physical movement and verbal interaction between the children and me and among the children themselves, I usually follow it with a quieter full class activity. Perhaps we will discuss our ongoing individual projects in science or social studies or we will read from the book we read aloud everyday. If the children have already had a lot of time to talk to each other, I will probably read aloud, which of course includes questions and discussion. At this point, if I have no real preference I will allow the children to vote on what they want to do next. Descriptions of how we read aloud and how we include content area subjects within the language arts block appear in detail later.

We review the homework for the day before within the context of the activity it complemented. If the homework centered on personality traits of a character in personal reading, we might discuss the traits during team reading, as a class right before silent reading or team reading. If the homework related to a script we are writing, we will discuss it as we continue work on the script:

Nina:	Okay, everyone put your homework in front of you. (Remember they have their homework at the corner of their desk so we waste no time digging in bookbags or fishing through desks.) Since we are going to work on the script, now let's hear the ideas you came up with last night.
Christian:	I said that we could have Brian work on science experiments that always mess up.
Nina:	What do you mean?
Christian:	Well like he invents shoes to make someone run faster, but when they put them on they go slower.
Nina:	Oh! I get it.
Peter:	Yea, maybe he can invent a pen that is suppose to do nice handwriting, then it leaks.
Nina:	Good. Other ideas about the problems and solutions in our play?

I use a variety of ways to monitor homework completion. The usual way is during the homework discussion. As the discussion proceeds, I quickly walk around the room to note who completed the homework and who did not. Sometimes I will just say, "Everyone raise up your homework." In this way I get a quick view of who did the homework. Also, children who did their homework receive attention and those who didn't don't. I may also quickly go down my class list: "When I call your name say 'yes' if you did your homework and 'no' if you didn't. If necessary, we have periodic discussions about how to help our peers remember their homework. (For example, call on the telephone to remind them, go to their house, and so forth). I plan to discuss homework assignments, and assessment will be discussed in each letter as it relates to the areas under discussion.

If I am constrained to a two-hour block of language arts, the bulk of the program concludes in the morning hours before lunch. Last year I was in a situation where I saw a group of children for only a half day before they switched to another teacher. So indeed, I had no choice but to do all I could do within two hours!

Here's how our schedule looked:

8:15–8:25	Children come in, organize desks, start writing daily entry in diaries.
8:25–8:35	Full school announcements.
8:35–8:45	Attendance and good morning activity; practice poem, parts of script, review homework.
8:45–9:45	Special area classes: art, physical education, music, library, or computers.
9:45–10:30	Writers' workshop including full class sharing.
10:30–11:15	Silent reading and team reading.
11:15–11:55	Read aloud; drama or poetry practice; individual social studies or science presentations.
11:55–12:00	Copy homework and Goodbye song.

As you can see we didn't have much time, and the few seconds we saved during transition time were valuable.

To end the day positively we usually pursue an activity similar to our morning activities. I might ask each child to tell me quickly what he or she will be working on in writing tomorrow, or I might ask the children to discuss their favorite part of the homework. These discussions usually take place when they are all on line ready to be dismissed. The children often want me to read one more chapter from our common book. This, too, brings us together as a community. If we are close to the poetry recital and we need practice we might end with a poem, but we often end with "Goodbye" by Gregg and Steve (1987).

Busy day, right? It is, but as I write to you about each component in more detail (—much more detail), I think you will realize that the children and I love what we do because the work is meaningful, creative and always personally challenging.

I'll write to you soon,

Nina

Nina

P.S. Have you noticed that whenever I share some of the conversation in my classroom I write "Nina" and also use the children's real names? Why do you think I do this and continue to do this in my subsequent letters? Think for a moment about my view of teacher education. Do you think I want you to use my exact words in your classroom? No. I am sharing my classroom with you, I am not giving you recipes to follow. Therefore, I avoid writing "Teacher" and "Student." This is my community and my story, and I expect you to think about my story in relation to yours. Teaching and learning happens within relationships not recipes.

LETTER #4
BROADENING OUR DEFINITIONS:
RETHINKING WHAT WE SAY ABOUT
OUR CHILDREN AND THEIR LEARNING

Dear Students,

Before we talk any further about my literacy community in the elementary school, I'd like to discuss some of the terms and definitions commonly used in literacy instruction. We need to think continually about the terms we use and the meanings we attach to them, for what we say and mean will influence our interactions with our students and their families. Our definitions influence both our interactions and the way our students and their families perceive them and their abilities. Have you ever heard a teacher or a parent say, "But he can't read"? I have, and it saddens me. Let me tell you a story:

Recently a third-grade child came into our classroom in the middle of the year. His worried mother told me that her son could not read. I tried to assure her that Aaron would do fine in this classroom because he would be part of a caring and helpful community. At least once a week, she would come by to ask how he was doing, and I always encouraged her to look at her son from a strengths perspective and begin to see that Aaron does read in his own way. She nodded hesitantly and I'm sure hoped for the best. I didn't need to hope though, because I was sure that Aaron would do well. In fact, I'm sure that all my students, given time, respect and consistency, will do fine because my definitions of reading and writing are broad and therefore encompass differing views of literacy success. After about three weeks, however, Aaron's mother decided to pull him out of our class and put him into a more traditionally structured class. She thought that our environment—with so many different activities, so much interaction, so much reading—distracted Aaron. I asked her to give Aaron more time, but she was convinced that he would be more successful in another classroom and he was moved.

According to our definition of "literacy" Aaron would have been successful. He would have begun to see himself as a reader and writer in his own right. He would have written what he was capable of writing and read what he was capable of reading. His literacy would have been supported and facilitated within an environment that allowed genuine purpose and meaning in all activities. Before I go into detail about my definitions of "literacy," I invite you to think of yours. What do you think has helped shape your definition? Is your definition broad enough to focus on not only form but also content and effect? Or is it narrowly focused on specific skills and products?

I believe that all children are literate because they are meaningful communicators. Indeed, children come to us as genuine communicators who have really already been involved in a miracle—the mastery of human communication. I am often awestruck by a young child's creative and natural use of language. Can you think of examples of such creative use? I can. My five-year-old son recently said to me, "Mom, I have a good remembery, right?" Once my 17-year-old at the age of three (I have a good remembery, too!) said, "Look Mommy apple juice is the same color as a fox." Wow! Have you ever heard a child say, "I broomed the floor," or "I goed to the store"? What do these examples illustrate about the natural development of language?

We can receive these utterances in two ways: from a strengths perspective or a deficit perspective. What might a teacher looking at them from a deficit view say? "I can't believe it. The kid doesn't even know the correct tense yet!" A teacher who views children from a strengths perspective might say, "Wow, This child has already learned that you add "-ed" to form the past tense!" Which teacher will you be?

As the children walk into my classroom, no matter their age or the traditional label they carry, I see them as literate. Literacy is more than just decoding or encoding print; it is communication. Literacy is creating and sending a message through dance, film, music, physical movement, talk, art and print. Can you think of other ways we create and send messages? If so, I would include them in my definition. Yes, we can treat even the blinking of a child's eyes or the squeezing of an adult's finger as literacy. If a child performs these physical actions to give a message, they are literate behaviors. Whenever I talk about this, I think about the time I took my Introduction to Special Education class to work once a week in a public school special education center. Many of the children we worked with were both physically and mentally challenged. The question that came after one visit was "Can all children learn?" The answer, of course, depends on your definition. Yes, all children can learn if your definition is broad enough. Learning for one child is finally being able to lift his or her head up or to respond with a signal when spoken to. Yes, that is quite a broad definition. But why do our definitions have to be narrow? When we broaden them we can include more people.

So can all children read? Can all children write? My answer is yes, they can. One child reads by talking about a book he is holding. Another reads when she strokes the pages of a book she loves to feel. (Actually, a lot of what I remember about my favorite books is the way the pages felt. I especially liked pages soft and thin and how the book smelled when I first opened it. I'm sure some of you, too, love the smell of new books. I guess it's kind of like people who like the smell of a new car—though usually a book is less expensive.) Another child writes as she listens to her friends talk about their ideas. She is also writes as she sits and thinks about what she should write. Indeed, as you will hear and see throughout these letters, I see reading and writing extending beyond mere static activities that result in predetermined products or results. Reading and writing are complex processes entwined in our human need to communicate and connect. Reading and writing are connection and relationship. One uses these processes to connect both to oneself and to others.

We all make these connections in different ways, at different times, in different places. In supportive environments, very young children naturally connect as their literacy emerges. Families immediately treat the new member of the family as a meaningful communicator. They respond to the child's cry as meaningful: Is she telling us that she's hungry? wet? tired? Think how excited we adults can become when the baby begins to say "mmmammammma." Do we say, "No! You can't talk yet! That's not how you say mommy! Say, "mommy"? Or do we declare "Oh, good you said Ma Ma"?

Have you ever heard a parent or caregiver tell a young child directly, "You do not know how to talk"? I've never heard this, though sadly I've often heard "Oh, he can't read yet." While families follow flexible definition of "talk" and "communication," these same children enter our traditional system of education to find themselves restricted by reductionistic definitions of "literacy." Authentic language learners at home have deficiencies at school. How do you think children feel when they hear they can't read or write? Have you ever been placed in such a position? Why would anyone need to put children in such positions of weakness? We should be appreciating our students' strengths. In fact, we ought to examine ourselves from a strengths perspective. When we are comfortable being positive about ourselves, we become comfortable looking at others in the same way. Broadening our definitions allows us to look positively on many more people. Broadening our definitions lets us see the strengths in ourselves and our students.

Moreover, definitions wide enough to include everyone influence our definition of success. With flexible and open definitions we can see all children as successful. This type of success is not based on comparing one child to another but on the unique knowledge each child possesses.

I can hear some of you saying to yourselves, "Yeah sure, this all sounds great about strengths. But don't we need to teach them what they don't know"? My first response is that we need to rethink our roles as teachers. If by "teaching," you mean distributing worksheets, teaching letters in isolation, demanding silence, then my answer is no, we don't need to teach. If by teaching, you mean setting up a supportive environment that encourages students and teachers to communicate and build their literacy expertise by connecting to important people within important activities, then I say yes.

This second type of teaching frees us from defining children by their weaknesses and allows us to build upon their expertise. That's right, we can build upon what the children come to us with and help facilitate their literacy growth. Notice I didn't say "teach literacy"; I said "facilitate." Children are literate beings, and our job is to help their natural literacy flourish. Does this mean that children won't move toward more standard literacy? Of course they will—but in their own time and space, using their own connections. Believe it or not, we need to do less teaching than we think. In fact, I contend that part of the so-called "student problem" is that we teach them too much and rarely leave them to think, explore and create.

When we see literacy from this natural and emergent perspective, traditional definitions fade from the scene. Teaching from this perspective, I realized that the hierarchical view of literacy—that is first children listen, then they speak, then they read and then they write—is far too simplistic. It is really ridiculous to believe that we can reduce such a complex human process to four separate sub-skills.

Unfortunately, this tendency to reduce, to label, to compartmentalize denies access to continued literacy growth to many of our children. Think about it. Many children receive labels because they are "two years below level" in reading.

(We'll talk about the question of levels and who fixes them later.) If we see literacy as hierarchical, these children should also be unready to write. I've heard so many times, "How can they write? They don't even know how to read!"

We need to rethink the idea that writing must wait for reading mastery. How have you, yourself, been taught to teach? Did we first introduce you to a concept abstractly or did we begin with concrete concepts? How did you learn addition? Did we just write 2+2 = ___ on the board, or did we encourage you to count beans, sticks, pennies? Ideally, we allow children to explore numbers through concrete manipulation of objects as they also learn the abstract symbols of corresponding numbers.

Let's transfer this idea to reading and writing. Which is more concrete, reading or writing? When children write (remember my definition of "writing" is broad so what I call "writing" is what you now might call scribbling or drawing) what do they hold in their hand? Is the act of writing more physical than the act of reading? Yes! Children touch and manipulate writing instruments as they press upon a writing surface. So which is more concrete? Why in the world have we believed for so long that reading should precede writing? As you will read in future letters, my students generally write before they read. In fact, many of my students experience first formal reading when they present their own written work. Don't worry, we'll talk later in more detail about this idea, too.

What are some of your definitions? Are they confining or expansive? Will your definitions help you treat children as meaningful communicators or will you attempt to fill them up before you consider them literate? Who will be successful in your classroom? Will you allow all children to feel successful or will you find "bright" children most closely matching your standard definitions? You need to reflect on these questions, for as I noted in the beginning of this letter, the definitions you choose influence both your interactions and the way your students and their families perceive them and their abilities. Your choice will, of course, ultimately be personal, but this choice will have a powerful influence on you, on all that occurs in your classroom and on the hearts of your students.

Sincerely,

Nina

Nina

P.S.   As you await my next letter I'd like you to think about the answers to these questions:

Why do you write?   Why do you read?
Who are you?   What are your strengths?
What do you think my next letter will be about writing or reading? Why?

LETTER #5
CHILDREN AS AUTHORS IN A WRITERS' WORKSHOP: RETHINKING "MY SUMMER VACATION"

Dear Students,

As you can see, I'm discussing writing before reading. Why do you think we're talking about writing first? Think for a moment about my last letter. Which really is more concrete? Writing is. Children grab a pencil, mark a paper, and start to tell their stories before they are forced to read someone else's. Indeed, it's easier to learn how to read your own writing because it's yours. In fact, most of the young writers I've had in my classroom have learned to read print with the books that they, themselves, have written. Luisa's first story was about her cat: "My cat is black. She is good." She wrote her story (remember my definition of writing is broad), I edited it, she put it in a book cover, and learned to read it as she shared her book with her friends. Sound simple? It is!

Before we talk about the concrete details of setting up a writers' workshop in your classroom, let's discuss some of the underlying basic principles. First of all, this program works children through a process all authors experience. Whether six or sixty, authors all go through the same process as they create. Therefore, when we implement writing process in the classroom the first principle we need to keep in mind is to see and treat all children as authors. The author's job is to write. Sometimes authors might write for themselves alone, as in diary writing, but more authors usually write for an audience. To reach this audience, an author needs to publish the work so that others can read it within and beyond the immediate community. Publication is, then, an integral part of a writing process program implemented in the classroom. With various forms of publication (homemade book covers, computer generated copy) available, children realize that they are authors. Without publication, creative writing loses one of its inherent purposes—communicating with others.

Now let's examine the specific details of implementing a writing process program.

Elements of a Writing Process Program

The following six fundamental elements make up a writing process program:

1. Time to write,
2. Control of topic choice,
3. Active student control,
4. Integration of sub-skills,
5. The right to an audience, and
6. Teacher-child conference.

Time to write. Children must have time to write every day. A 20- or 30-minute daily writing period instills in children the habit of writing and gives them the confidence to develop fluency and practice skills. This is the minimal time necessary to allow children work on first drafts, to edit and revise their drafts, and to publish their final copy as hardcover books. A 20- or 30-minute writing period also gives children the time to confer with their friends and teacher and to absorb new ideas before revising, editing and publishing. This daily commitment to writing communicates to the children the significance of writing in the curriculum and enables them to integrate and automate writing sub-skills.

Control of topic choice. If children enjoy considerable freedom in choosing their topic, they realize that what they have to say, not only what the teacher assigns, is important. While initially some children faced with the task of choosing their own topic experience frustration, ideas will come easier after sharing and questions from peers and teacher. Topic ideas also come easier after the students listen to some children's literature and discuss such techniques as choice of subject, characters, the title and word choice.

Here are some suggestions to pass along to students having difficulty with story ideas:

-Think about personal experiences.
-Think about subjects you know a lot about.
-Go to the library and look at other book topics.
-Interview classmates for topic ideas.
-Discuss possible topics with family members and use these ideas in school.
-Keep an idea list in your writing folder.
-Use the idea list posted in the classroom.

Active student control. When children have the time and opportunity to choose and develop personal topics, they begin to feel some control over the writing process. This feeling of control, in turn, helps them learn that the influence of their choices extends beyond their work to the classroom environment. When they see their writing and opinions are in a supportive atmosphere, they become more willing to take risks and their writing skills develop. They connect their writing to their personal work, activities and social interactions. In time, they become less passive, more independent, and begin to make their own decisions. Their control over decisions produces the desire and motivation to learn and be active participants in the writing process.

Integration of sub-skills. Another useful element of writing process is the freedom to focus on one aspect of the writing at a time and thus keep from being overwhelmed by the need to immediately address every sub-skill: spelling, legibility, punctuation and sequential and creative sentences. The following four steps of writing process aid in developing these sub-skills:

1. *The first draft.* Children writing first drafts learn to focus on their ideas and not worry about spelling, punctuation, handwriting and so on. I encourage invented spelling and give priority to exploring thoughts, ideas

and feelings, avoiding mechanical rules for the time being. When children begin to feel safe about using words and realize that invented spelling helps them write down their ideas, they become confident writers who willingly dare to continue their writing growth.

2. *Revision of the draft.* During the revision stage, the children continue to shape their content by sharing with their peers and me and clarifying and receiving ideas for story development. In this stage of the writing process, the main idea, that is to say, the selection of a title, the sequence, and the concept of reality and fantasy are developed and refined. Their peers and I contribute ideas to help with the revision of the draft.

3. *Editing.* In the editing stage, when the draft is being prepared for publication, instruction in mechanical skills takes place. Spelling is standardized; punctuation is corrected, and capitalization is discussed and corrected. This type of instruction invites the children to learn these skills in the context of their own work. They begin to understand that the purpose of such skills is to communicate their stories effectively.

4. *Publication.* During the publication stage, the children cut and fold paper to the measurement of pre-made covers and transfer their corrected draft onto the pages of their new book. At this point, handwriting skills are taught and reinforced, and children learn that legible handwriting is another advantageous part of effective communication.

The right to an audience. Another key element of the writing process is sharing the work, which achieves an integration of all the earlier stages. Given the opportunity to share their work with an audience, children learn that the essence of writing is communication. Their writing skills become meaningful and they feel in control. Also, helping to develop the work of their peers enhances their self-esteem. This is why sharing with another child, the teacher, and the whole class is a crucial step in the writers' workshop.

I use the acronym TAG at the beginning of the year to help children receive the work of others positively. This simple acronym helps the children remember these three rules: (1) T—Tell what you like, (2) A—Ask questions, and (3) G—Give ideas. At first, I require my children to follow the rules strictly but once they establish the TAG habit, I allow them to discuss the work of their peers more informally. The effect TAG produces is so positive that it continues even after I stop actively reinforcing it.

Teacher-child conference. Perhaps the most critical element of the writing process is the teacher-child conference. These conferences can take place during the creation of the first draft, revising, editing or sharing. They should last from about three to seven minutes and should concentrate on only one specific skill at a time. Therefore, if the child is working on the initial draft or its revision, the conference should address only questions of content. When the child is editing, the conversation should center on the mechanics. At the publication stage of the process, comments should address handwriting. This conference behavior helps both the student and teacher, focusing on the one skill at a time, avoid being overwhelmed by too many ideas and corrections at once.

The type of questions that you use during conferences is very important. The questions should never remove control from the writer but should convey your trust in the child's own judgment. Such questions as "What are your concerns?" and "Could you tell me a little more?" are appropriate because they encourage the pupil, not you, to talk. Such questions also demonstrate your genuine belief in and respect for the child.

Implementation of Writers' Workshop

Once you have decided to teach writing as a process, you should commit yourself to the following ten principles:

1. Be consistent and committed. Schedule writing *every* day at the same time and set aside a generous amount of time, like 20 or 30 minutes. This regularity allows writing to develop out of habit into exciting anticipation.
2. Allow the children to control the topic. Avoid assigning topics. Assigning topics, even "on just the first day to give them an idea," makes it harder for the child. It reinforces passivity and the impression that what the teacher thinks is most important. Be calm. Topic ideas will come out of sharing with peers and the reading of children's literature.
3. Remember, writing is a process. A finished product will not emerge after every writing period. Be patient and accepting. Let the children think, experiment, and feel at ease within the process.
4. Sit and write with the students at least once a week. You can also bring in writing that you have worked on outside the classroom and share places where you've had difficulties. This could be done during whole class sharing time as the children respond to your writing with TAG. This behavior reinforces the idea that writing is important to everyone.
5. Promote a literate environment in your classroom. With an opportunity to use a variety of writing and reading materials—pens, pencils, markers, crayons, an assortment of paper, books, magazines, newspapers —the child will become comfortable with these communication tools. When children find themselves surrounded by literacy—by the trappings of authorship— they begin to feel at home as authors.
6. Keep the children in control during all phases of the process with questions and behaviors that exhibit respect for their decision-making ability. Say, "What do you think your title is going to be?" not, "Why don't you use this title?"
7. Smile (even if it take some practice) when a child hands you a smudged and wrinkled first draft. Remember what really counts are the ideas and that you positively accept the child's writing.
8. Teach necessary skills within the context of the child's own work and during the appropriate stage of the process. For example, discuss handwriting when it is important—during publishing —not during the first draft. This approach allows a child to focus on one aspect at a time instead of being overwhelmed by everything at once.

9. Allow the children to share with their peers every day. This sharing encourages topic ideas, gives the child an audience to use as a resource, enables the child to be a resource and maintains a child's control over the activity.

10. Take it easy! In the beginning it may seem as though nothing is happening. But little by little through daily, consistent writing, conferences and sharing, those once-isolated skills will form a meaningful whole in the mind of the child encouraged to write.

On the First Day

One of the most often-asked and most difficult questions is how to start: What do you do on the first day of implementation of the writing process program? The following 15 guidelines will help you get the first day off to a good start.

1. Tell your students that every day at this time the class will be writing.
2. Give them all a piece of paper and ask them to write.
3. Sit down and write with them.
4. After about five minutes get up and circulate around the room, speaking to your students about what they are writing. Spend only a few seconds or so with each child to give encouragement. ("Wow, I really like how you started working so quickly.")
5. After about ten minutes allow the children to share their work with or listen to the work of a friend.
6. You circulate around the room too and model sharing behavior so that the children can hear you. ("I really liked the part about your dog barking.")
7. After about five minutes of this individual sharing, call the class together again as a whole. ("Okay everyone, let's all move to our seats now.")
8. Introduce full-class sharing by asking if anyone who would like to share their writing with the whole class.
9. Allow the children to comment on the shared work by telling what they liked, asking questions and giving ideas. Model this behavior by being an active participant.
10. Allow a few more children to share in front of the class before ending the writing period.
11. Comment on how well you thought the writing went, giving specific praise to individual students. ("I really liked the way Melvin listened while Kyli was sharing her story.")
12. Give all the children manila folders for their writing. Explain that these folders are for them to keep their writing in and they should take them out during every writing period. Briefly point out that drafts will eventually be published in book form. Show the children some covers and samples.
13. Take it easy and take it slow. Don't try to cover all the concepts of the program in one day.
14. Follow these steps consistently so that they become automatic to the children.

15. Make writing positive and enjoyable so that you and your students will want to write again tomorrow.

Now that we've discussed an overview of the writing program, let's start listening to some of the conversations that take place between these student authors, their peers and their teacher. First I'll present samples of dialogue that typically occur during the first month of implementation and then show examples of dialogue that extend over the school year. These samples come from my classroom transcripts and are therefore genuine interactions. Of course, we'll discuss each piece and reflect upon the contextual and instructional components necessary for the successful implementation of a writing process program.

First Day: Introduction of the Writing Process to the Full Class

Nina: We are going to write about anything we want. What do we call people who write stories?

Jake: Authors.

Nina: Where do authors get their ideas?

Matt: From looking around; from things in our family; from things we do; from other people.

Nina: That reminds me. There is one word we can use to talk about "things that happen to us." It starts with "ex."

Veronica: Exercises.

Nina: That's a really good try. I was thinking about the word "experiences." Authors write about their experiences. Some authors write make-up, pretend experiences, too.

John: Yes, people can write about their childhood. When you are adults you can write about your childhood.

Nina: That's right. We can write about our memories sometimes. Okay. Now when we begin to write—when you get an idea—what do you do when you don't know how to spell a word?

Beth: Sound it out.

Nina: Well, what if when you sound it out, you still can't think of the first letter, what are you going to do?

Annie: Ask somebody.

Nina: That's true you can ask somebody. In the first draft, what is important are your ideas. If you get up and ask somebody you may forget your ideas. Now give me a big word.

Neil: Massachusetts.

Nina: Massachusetts . . . [M] . . . Oh, great! I have a great idea and I don't want to stop to think of all those letters, so I'll put an "M." Then what can I do if I don't want to write any of the other letters?

Mara: Leave a blank.

Nina: That's right! That's what I do when I don't want to worry

about spelling. I leave a blank. Let's all write. All of us are
going to write because all people write.

And we write. During implementation on the first day, I sit in the community of
student writers as they write. Then after about five minutes or so, I get up and go
to every single child and give them each a positive, encouraging comment like:

"I see you have already started writing."
"You have a lot to say."
"Don't worry about handwriting."
"Oh, you don't need to erase. Just cross it out and go on. We are not worried
about how it looks."
"I see you aren't worried about spelling. You just put a blank right there."
"I like how you are not afraid to write this word."

To Mandy who drew a house:
"Now tell me something about this house."

I continue to circulate and when I come back to Mandy, I see she has written
something in invented spelling.

Nina:	Wow, Mandy, you've written something. Tell me what it says.
Mandy:	A man lives in this house.
Nina:	That's great. The story goes with your picture.

I picked up a student's draft and addressed the whole class.

Nina:	Everyone listen for one minute. Marco is looking right at me. I know that he is ready to listen. Now I see that everyone is listening. What do we call this? This is what we first work on when we begin to write.
Tim:	A rough draft
Nina:	I call it a first draft, but some people call it a rough draft. Where did you hear that language?
Tim:	From my other teacher.
Nina:	That's good. What is most important when we do a first draft? (No response.) Okay, what is not important when we write a first draft? Remember, what don't we have to worry about when we write a first draft?
Natalie:	Spelling.
Nina:	That's right. And another thing we don't worry about is handwriting. Now what is important in a first draft?
Marilyn:	Your story.
Nina:	That's right. What is most important is your idea, your story. Go back to writing. Thank you for letting me interrupt you.

The children write for about five more minutes as I continue to talk individually with each child.

Nina:	Let's get back together as a class.
Luke:	Wait. I'm not finished.
Nina:	Oh, let's talk about what authors do. What authors do you all read?
Jack:	*Amelia Bedelia.*
Nina:	Oh! I read a lot of *Amelia Bedelia* too.
Dee:	*Ralph and the Motorcycle* (the Beverly Cleary book)
Nina:	How long do you think it took Beverly Cleary to write that book?
Sara:	A year?
Mary:	5 years?
Tania:	5 months?
Nina:	Yes, different authors take different amounts of time to do their writing. I'm a slow writer. So it takes me a long time to write. So do you think we need to finish our story today?
Carl:	No.
Nina:	What are we going to do with our drafts?
Warren:	Save them.
Nina:	That's right. Authors save their drafts so they can work on them the next day. Since you are all authors now, we are going to write every day. So we need to save our drafts. I'm going to give each one of you a folder to keep your drafts in. This is called your writing folder. Tomorrow when it is writing time, the first thing you'll do is take out your writing folder.

Discussion of First Day

The preceding passage illustrates the way I begin the writing process in my classroom. While of course some of the dialogue will vary and the amount of time spent in writing will change according to the age of the children, the foundational principles remain the same. As I've said, a writer is a writer no matter how old or how young. Therefore, we use the same vocabulary all writers use. You'll notice that in this transcript of the first day I avoided a lecture on the writing process, but I began to teach it within the context of the children's work. So, for example, the children learned the word "draft" during the time they were actually working on a draft. In this way, they receive an introduction to the vocabulary in the context of its meaningful use. My goal on the first day of writing is not to have students memorize the process. It is to give them a feel for what they will be doing every day in our class and help them feel safe and excited about writing. On the first day, I want them to feel like authors though, so I consciously make sure to

- talk to them as authors,
- connect them to professional authors (like Beverly Cleary),
- use questions to encourage active responses throughout discussion and
- use open-ended questions (like "Can you tell me about it?") to keep them in control of their own work.

I also illustrate for them the whole process, including sharing and publication, so they begin to understand the purpose of writing. On the first day I adjust my schedule to ensure enough sharing time. I also make sure to show the empty hard covers so that children can immediately imagine their writing piece in published form. In fact, during the first class, I make sure I get at least one child to publish a book. The length of this publication will of course vary with the student. For example, a published book for one kindergartner could easily be "I love my Mommy." The product is not important here. What is important is that this child feels like an author and that his or her work gets published even if it is only one sentence. Once students see this first completed publication they become very eager to get their own work published as quickly as possible.

Let me make something very clear: A teacher should respond to an author's first written piece with great care. We want all our children to feel safe and accepted. Therefore, we must receive their written work with respect. Your first goal is to make sure that your students understand that you value what they write and consider it important. I convey this respect in my classroom by trying to ensure that all my students publish their first piece no matter what it might be. Remember, authors write every day and generally have plenty of time to develop, refine and edit their stories. The first day or week or, for some children, month is not the time to be particularly critical or perfectionistic. It is the time to help all your students feel like authors as they publish their first books.

Let's take what may look for a moment like a sharp turn to making book covers. But you'll be amazed at the power of these book covers. Some teachers decide not to introduce publication until their children can write "complete stories." In these classrooms, students miss the full view of the process and lose the motivational push that publication gives them. Before you introduce the writing process to your class, take the time to make these covers. The harder the cardboard the better since the closer the resemblance student-authored books bear to real books, the more authentic their authorship will seem. I also suggest that you place your students' books in your regular class library so that they see their work included with the work of the professional authors they read. In this way, their personal perception of authorship continues to strengthen.

Making Book Covers

Materials
    17"x 12" piece contact paper
    Two 6"x 9" pieces of cardboard
    Scissors
    Glue (a glue stick is easiest and neatest)

Writing paper (8 1/2" x 11")

Procedure
1.   Place contact paper sticky side up and glue the two pieces of cardboard, side by   side in the center. Leave approximately half an inch space between the two   pieces of cardboard.
2.   Cut the corners of the contact paper off and fold sides over onto the cardboard.

Inside of book
1.   Fold two blank sheets of paper under three sheets of writing paper.
2.   Fold in half and staple.

Inside and cover
1.   Put glue on the back flap inside the cover previously made.
2.   Place folded (stapled) sheets, inside the cover and close the cover. Open and adjust papers for opening and closing the book.

The Publishing Table

During the second half of the writers' workshop year, I encourage children from first to third grade and older to make their own covers. By this time, I have begun to encourage the children to choose only their best work for publication. Once they feel safe as authors, we no longer rush into publishing but take it slower. But now we can devote time to allow students to make their own covers. Place on the table the following materials:

> cut pieces of contact paper,
> cut pieces of cardboard,
> glue or glue sticks and
> paper.

After they have edited, proofread and written their final copy children can make their book covers.

At this point, let me present a transcript of an initial sharing session, which usually takes place every day after the children have written for about 20 minutes. I like to use sharing as the closing activity every day because it brings the class together and gives the full class access to the work of their peers. On the first day, I ask for volunteers to share their work in front of the room. From the second day onward, children sign up to share their work on a weekly sign-up sheet. I encourage children to share no matter where they are in the process. They might share an initial draft, a title or a fully published work. Teachers who share only published copy, final copy put in a book cover, in front of an audience send two unfortunate messages: first, that the product is most important, not the process (remember this is writing *process*); and second, that an author need not use his or her audience during the process. Like most professional writers, our authors need an audience to help with the refinement of the piece of writing. When a work is already published, the audience's ideas can no longer influence the writing.

Nina: Now that we all have our folders for our drafts, let's come together as a class so we can share our work. Who would like to share? (No response.)

I know sometimes it might be a little scary to share but in this class it won't be because we do something called **TAG** (I write TAG on the board from top to bottom):

T

A

G

(I then say) This helps everyone feel happy to share. Who can guess what T stands for? (No response.)

It's "tell." What would we tell someone about their story so they feel good about it?

Derek: Something nice.

Nina: That's right! We are going to tell them what we liked about the story. T means "Tell what you like." (I write this on the board after the letter T.) Good! Now what do you think A might stand for? (No response.)

When we want to find out about something, what do we do?

Colleen: We ask.

Nina: Good, and that's what we do after we listen to someone's story. We ask them about things in the story. A stands for "Ask questions." (I write this on the board after the letter A.) Now can anyone guess what G stands for? (No response.)

When we want to help someone with their writing we can give them what?

Alonzo: Ideas.

Nina: That's right, and that's what G means. After we listen to our friend's story we can "Give them ideas or suggestions" (I write this on the board after the letter G.) to help them with the story. Now everyone let's say this. I'll say it first; then you say it:

T Tell what you like.

All: T Tell what you like.

Nina: A Ask questions.

All: A Ask questions.

Nina: G Give ideas.

All: G Give ideas.

Nina: Good. Now who would like to share? (A few students raise their hands. I choose one at random.)

You know today I am choosing a student today but after this I am not going to choose anymore. We're going to have a sign-up sheet so that when you want to share, you can sign your name under the day you want to share. So what day is tomorrow?

Shanika: Tuesday.
Nina: That's right, so let me make the sign-up sheet now. Watch. (I take a piece of paper and put the days of week on the paper with lines underneath so that children can see):

Tuesday

_____

_____

_____

Wednesday

_____

_____

_____

Thursday

_____

_____

_____

Friday

_____

_____

_____

Nina: So now whenever you want to share, you can sign up where there's space and if there's no space that's ok because there will be a new sign-up sheet every week. You can sign up whenever you want, but do you think everyone can be at the sign-up sheet all at once?
Marlon: No.
Nina: Why not?
Becca: It will get too crowded.
Nina: That's right. So the rule is only three people at one time near the sign-up sheet. I'll hang it right here so you can reach it to sign up later. Let's begin sharing. Come on up, Derek. Now before you start reading your story, I want you to look around and make sure everyone is looking at you. Now recognize someone who is sitting appropriately. (No response.)
              Who is sitting nicely and ready to listen?
Derek: Chris.
Nina: Good. Now say, "Chris is sitting nicely and ready to listen."
Derek: Chris is sitting nicely and ready to listen.
Nina: Good. Now recognize someone else.
Derek: Amy you're sitting nicely.
Nina: Excellent! Now begin sharing.
Derek: (He reads from his draft.) I like Jessica. I like Randy. I like my Mommy.
Nina: (Claps.) Excellent reading, Derek. Everyone give Derek a hand. Good. Now let's do TAG. What does T stand for?

Carrie:	Tell what you like.
Nina:	That's right. Now someone raise your hand and tell Derek what you liked about his story. (Hands go up.) Now, Derek, you choose someone.
Derek:	Jessica?
Jessica:	I liked your whole story.
Nina:	Good, Jessica. What part did you like the best?
Jessica:	When he said my name.
Nina:	Oh! It is nice to hear your name. Does anyone have any questions for Derek about his story? (No response.) (Teacher puts her hand up and Derek chooses her.)
Nina:	Why do you like the people in your story?
Derek:	Because they're my friends.
Nina:	Oh, good. Maybe tomorrow you can add that to your story "because they are my friends." Give Derek a hand for sharing, everyone. Derek, thank you for being the first one to share. Now you get to choose someone else to share. Raise your hand if you'd like to be the next one to share. Derek, now you can choose.

Usually I allow three children to share during the first session. If the class as a whole is attentive and eager, I might allow one or two more. I also try to include a child who has published the first day so that the class gets a good view of the book cover. Remember, these first published books might only be two or three sentences, so I can help one child revise, edit and publish during the first writing session. After the first child shares and the students see how TAG helps the work receive positive responses, most children clamor to share and even become upset when sharing time ends. Because they write every day, children realize quickly that they will have many opportunities to share. As you noticed, too, I help the children take over the session and run it themselves. But notice, as well, how I specifically guided their responses. I guide them through the steps of TAG and how to respond to their peers' work (applause) and how they praise each other ("Michael is ready to listen"). I also immediately allow the first child to choose the next child to share. These techniques powerfully create and support a positive classroom and encourage children to recognize each other actively. In fact, our only problem is that everyone wants to recognize everyone. An easy way to curtail this effusion is say "Recognize three people for the way they are sitting/looking at you/ready."

As you saw, the previous dialogue briefly touched upon many of the sharing rules. I elaborate upon and reinforce these rules during the whole first week so that all the children become comfortable with them. Certain rules emerge through their use of the sign-up sheet. One rule already mentioned is that only three people at a time are allowed at the sheet. Reinforced consistently, the rule avoids problems of pushing, crowding and arguing. With many of my classes, I include a rule about signing up in pen. I have found some children so eager to share in front of the class that they erase other children's names when no more blank lines are available. Sometimes they even add their own blanks. Writing in pen helps prevent alterations.

Another lesson emerges from this sign-up sheet when we talk about writing or erasing only our own names and the need to make sure everyone gets a chance to share at least once a week. Therefore, a rule like "We only share once per week" emerges. The number of blanks under each day of the week varies according to the amount of time you can devote to sharing. I usually provide six blanks a day to make sure that each child in a class of thirty has a chance to share once a week. As time passes and children become familiar with the schedule, I become more flexible with the order of the process. If for some reason we have insufficient time for all the children signed up to share, we might start with full-class sharing before breaking up to work on our writing pieces. When we fall behind in the full-class sharing, we might extend the time a little to catch up. This flexibility is possible when students feel secure and safe as authors in the classroom. But one thing is certain: they will never let you forget sharing time!

It is crucial that the rules of writing process remain clear and consistent. With this consistency, children become independent and feel secure with my expectations. During the first week of writing process, we create rules together as a class. As with all class created rules, the teacher should understand the principles the rules are based on and guide the children as they create rules that correspond to these principles. The eleven general writing process rules that guide us follow here. In each class the specific wording may differ, but the underlying philosophy remains intact.

Writers' Workshop

1.   Write three different first drafts.
2.   Pick one draft to publish.
3.   Self-edit your draft.
4.   Ask a friend to edit your draft.
5.   Take your draft to an adult to edit.
6.   Write your final copy.
7.   Read over your final copy and make corrections.
8.   Give a friend your final copy to make corrections.
9.   Give an adult your final copy to make corrections.
10.   Put your final copy in a cover.
11.   Share, help others and go back to step 1.

Now here's a chance for you to see exactly how interactions in writers' workshop might proceed. These are not scripts for you to follow, however, since you'll want to interact in your own way.

Josef During Full Class Sharing at the End of the First Month of Implementation

Josef shared his story and the class responded with TAG (tell what you like, ask questions, give ideas):

Nina: How can Josef give us more information?
Mario: More detail.
Nina: That's good. How else? (No response.) What about his friends? What could he do to give us more information?
Mandy: They could say something.
Nina: That's right. His friends could talk. That's called dialogue. Josef what could your friends say when they walk into your house?
Josef: Hi!
Nina: Good, that's dialogue.

Discussion

Here I work with Josef on a revision of his draft. Notice that we are not talking about the mechanics of the piece but about its content. Here I am pushing Josef to become more fluent in his writing by adding more details and dialogue. I make sure during the next writing session to hold Josef accountable for making these revisions on this piece. Either I would confer with him directly, or in advance I would ask a student to work with him (for example, "Jessica, since you have dialogue in your story, would you help Josef with his tomorrow?").

I might also ask Josef who he would like to have help him the next day. This way Josef remains in control. If he happens to choose someone without much experience with this type of revision, I would say "Josef, I know that you like to work with ____. But for this skill you need to choose someone who has already used it in their own writing."

Loretta

Nina: What are you writing, Loretta?
Loretta: My story.
Nina: Are you writing your first draft?
Loretta: It's going in a book cover.
Nina: You're publishing it?
Loretta: Yes.
Nina: Okay. You're in publication. Say, "I'm in publication."
Loretta: I'm in publication.
Nina: What will you be working on tomorrow?

Discussion

Here I am conferring with Loretta during the first week of writers' workshop. I usually confer with children at their own desks and maintain no separate conference area. This way, I am always in the community and monitoring others as I confer. Here I encourage Loretta to use the vocabulary of a writer. So when she says "story" I push her to refine her meaning. When she says that "it's in a book" I give her the appropriate word "publication" to use and model the appropriate sentence. As a result, the children learn an author's vocabulary within the context of their own work and when it is most meaningful to them. When I use a writer's vocabulary consistently during writing workshop, the children begin to speak as authors, too. I also asked Loretta what she will be working on after publication. This sends the clear message that authors continue to write after publication and they write every day.

Full Class Lesson

Nina: Jessica, I really liked how your story was complete. (To the class) What are some of the reasons that I say her story is complete? What does her story have? (No response.) Does her story have a beginning?

Wayne: Yes.

Nina: What else—a story has a beginning—Alvin?

Alvin: And an end.

Nina: That's right. It has an end. And what else does it have?

Mike: A middle.

Nina: Good. Jessica's story has a beginning, a middle and an end. What's the beginning?

Sam: She has a teacher.

Nina: Good. What's the middle?

Harry: He leaves.

Nina: What's the end?

Fran: He comes back.

Nina: Jessica also has something in her story that most complete stories have . . . a problem and a _____? (No response.) What word goes along with problem? When we solve a problem what is that called?

Nate: Solution.

Nina: That's right. Jessica's story has a problem and a solution. What's the problem?

Genna: The teacher leaves.

Nina: Good. What's the solution?

Marco: The teacher comes back.

Nina: That's right. They go to complain to the principal and the teacher they like comes back. What an excellent story, Jessica!

Discussion

Here we have an example of a contextualized lesson. I used Jessica's story as a vehicle to teach five basic aspects of a narrative piece: beginning, middle, end, problem and solution. Notice that my lesson emerged through questioning. I began with an open-ended question and then if children needed support, I narrowed the question until a child found the answer. Throughout the lesson I connected the major concepts to Jessica's story (for example, "Good. Jessica's story has a beginning, a middle, and an end. What's the beginning?"). Thus, I kept the instruction within the context of meaningful written work.

In subsequent individual writing conferences I connect with this full class lesson as I urge children to include these basic elements in their own stories. During full-class sharing, too, these concepts become reinforced as we listen to other pieces and talk about their beginnings, middles and ends. Questions to encourage such reflection might include, What is the problem of your story? Have you thought about a solution, yet? If you think about a solution will it be easier for you to get to an end of your story?

Timothy: An Idea for a Draft

Timothy had a hard time writing. He could formulate no ideas. So I stopped the class and asked each child what he or she was working on. As the session went on, Timothy still hesitated to mark the paper. Here's what happened:

Nina:	Timothy, I want to see you write something. I'll be back in three minutes. (I left him. When I returned I saw that he had written his name.) Okay. Now you need to continue. Mark your paper. (About ten minutes later I approached him again.)
Timothy:	I have an idea.
Nina:	What?
Timothy:	My friends.
Nina:	Good. What letter do you think you should write to begin the word "My"?
Timothy:	Z.
Nina:	Good. Write it down. Now what letter for friend? (He hesitated, then struggled to make the letter "T." After that he wrote a few more letters and stopped.)
Nina:	Now tell me what that says.
Timothy:	My friends are nice. I play with my friends.
Nina:	That's great. Are you finished?
Timothy:	Yes. I want to share.
Nina:	Do you want to practice reading it first?
Timothy:	Yes. (He began to read.)

Discussion

Timothy, like many writers, got stuck for an idea. To help him generate ideas, I stopped the class and asked each child what he or she was working on. This sends Timothy the clear message that he need not depend only on me, his teacher, for ideas. He can get help from his friends. I was also working to reduce his reluctance to mark the paper. He was hesitant and so needed the direct instructions to "mark the paper." Allowing him the time and declining to do it for him was extremely important. I wanted him to learn that it was his work, he is the author, and it is his job to write. Therefore, I continued to push him to write *something*. I refrained from correcting him when he said "Z" for "My" because at this point it was important for him to mark the paper no matter what he wrote. Of course, when he writes his final copy for publication, I address standard spelling. The minute Timothy finished his story, I asked him to tell me about it. When he did, I wrote down the words he dictated. I did not mark his paper until he did. In this way the message is loud and clear: He is the author and I am only the editor.

Timothy in Publication

Nina: Let's go, Timothy, pick up your pencil and start writing now. Here, write the "F." Good, line down, now make the lines across. Hurry up now, and concentrate. Make your "r" now . . . right next to the "F." Good, now make the "i." You do that letter well. Now, write the "e."
(Timothy listened and performed the tasks exactly as directed. At times I talked briefly about letter formation.) Start at the top line then go down. Good. Now make the circle. (Sometimes I guided his pencil. Other times I formed the letters for him. I was firm and my directions continued to be short and to the point. Timothy finished his book and then read his story into the tape. I quickly got a cover for him and stapled in his final copy.)

Discussion

Only when Timothy started his final copy did we begin to talk about handwriting. Handwriting is important in the publication because this is what others must be able to read. Some young children can copy a whole edited draft for publication while others need more guidance. I had Timothy write some letters, but to avoid frustrating him, I wrote some of the letters. We need to make sure that while we facilitate children's progress we do it in such a way that they feel as though they have accomplished something. Timothy had time to practice his writing so that when he shared his work with the class, he felt successful and proud.

April Starts a Draft

April was having trouble starting a new draft. I encouraged her to walk around to see what the others were doing. Then I remembered that she had gotten an idea from Tory for her last poem.

Nina: April, you know how to get ideas from your friends. You're good at that. Remember you got that idea to start your poem from Tory?
April: (Nodded yes.)
        (Later I noticed that she had written a good amount of text.)
Nina: You're really writing! You look really happy!
Tory: She's happy because I'm drawing her pictures for her.

Discussion

April had great difficulty getting ideas and frequently tried to push me for ideas. Here I praised April and recognized her for seeking ideas from her peers. This constant recognition and reinforcement develops a true community of writers not only dependent on the teacher but willing and able to seek guidance from their classmates as well. Notice that along with me, all the community members become active participants responsible for the writers' workshop.

Alvin Begins a Revision

Alvin needed to focus as he wrote the names in his family:

Nina: What can you say about some of those people in your family? (No response.)
        Tell me something about your Mom.
Alvin: My Mom and Dad sleep together.
Nina: Good, write that down. (Alvin finished a story about where everybody slept in his house. There was a sentence about Cindy, who is not part of his family.) Should this sentence be in this story?
Alvin: No.
Nina: Why?
Alvin: Because she isn't part of my family.
Nina: Good. Your title is "My Family." But could we say a little more about what this story is about? What is it about your family that you talk about in this story?
Alvin: Where they sleep.
Nina: So could you put that in the title? (No response.)
Nina: Think of a title with the word "sleep" in it.
Alvin: "Where My Family Sleeps."

Nina: Good, that title tells us more about what the story is about.

Discussion

This passage comes from a conference with Alvin where we worked on creating and expanding the main idea. I accepted what Alvin had written and then helped him to expand. Therefore, the list of names turned into a story about his family. What Alvin, the author, wrote was never negated but elaborated upon to help him write a more complete narrative. Even he deleted one sentence from his draft; he deleted it as a result of questioning—"Should this sentence be in this story?"—so Alvin remained in control of his story. This approach is extremely important when we revise a child's work. Remember it is their work, not yours; therefore, the essence of the story must remain. Notice that while I helped Alvin refine his title, I did it so that Alvin kept the decision-making power—"Think of a title with the word 'sleep' in it"—and while I guided his decision, it remained his decision as the author.

Assessment Issues

Assessment and evaluation in a writers' workshop involves two major principles: One, we evaluate a skill during the stage of writing where it is most meaningful; and two, we evaluate student writers according to their individual growth, not in comparison with other writers.

Therefore, as I mentioned earlier, I avoid discussions and assessments of handwriting when a child is working on a draft. This would be inappropriate since in a draft the child needs to focus on the content. I discuss and evaluate handwriting during the writing of the final copy since this is when legibility becomes meaningful. Discussions of standard spelling and such other features of language as punctuation marks and noun-verb agreement are most meaningful as the child edits, so this is when I assess these language skills. If I assess these skills during the creation of the draft, I might inhibit creativity and incorrectly stress the importance of form over content.

Children should be assessed according to their own individual progress and not compared to others. Therefore, you should defer any formal "grade collection" until you know each child and what he or she can do. After you have a few pieces of writing, you can begin to monitor progress as you look back and look ahead during the process of writing. Meanwhile, any evaluation in writers' workshop should encourage and move a writer along in his or her own development. As I evaluate this development, it helps me to focus on these five stages of the process: the draft, the revision, editing, sharing, and publication.

The draft. At this point, I can evaluate fluency as I look at the length of drafts over time for each individual writer. A child who goes from a two-sentence draft to a five-sentence draft in two weeks has made admirable progress in fluency. I can also evaluate the range of topics written about over time and infer various grades from this skill. Therefore, a child who writes about dogs for three weeks, then moves on to another subject shows progress as he or she works with new topics.

The revision. During revision children usually expand upon ideas and incorporate dialogue, adjectives, details and so forth. I can monitor a child's use of these techniques over time and evaluate his or her work in the context of personal growth. I can also infer grades as I watch children revise with each other and listen to the advice they give their peers.

Editing. At this point, we concentrate on standard spelling and such other language features as punctuation marks and tense forms. As children self-edit their work, I can derive grades from what they add and what they delete. The editing stage is where I help children work on specific skills. For example, if I see that a child needs to work on punctuation at the end of a sentence, I will help correct all other aspects of the draft and then have the child try to punctuate each sentence individually (for example, "Derek, now I want you to go and read each sentence and try to put all the periods where they belong."). I can, therefore, obtain a grade from within the context of personal writing.

From edited copy, in fact, students get their individual spelling words to study. And so spelling grades come directly from each child's individual writing pieces. I'll write more about how and why I pursue individualized spelling in a subsequent letter that focuses on general assessment issues.

Sharing. During sharing I can easily determine an oral development grade as I monitor a child's expression, voice quality and confidence over time. Again, I evaluate each child within the context of their own progress and resist comparing them to others. In this way, a child remains successful as he or she grows in writing ability.

Publication. As mentioned earlier, I can use handwriting and the final publication (including the neatness of the book cover and the illustrations) to determine grades. But we need to be careful about what "standard" we use to decide what is legible. It might be appropriate to push one child to rewrite a publication for legibility two times, but another child so treated might reach the point of frustration. This is where, again, your knowledge of your children and their individual strengths and abilities will help you be successful in appropriately assessing your young authors. Your goal, remember, is to help them be successful in writing workshop.

Before I close, let me emphasize how important it is to make sure you enjoy writing. Your excitement and enthusiasm about writing will be a powerful force that drives the program. Maybe you can publish a book you can share with your students! Maybe you could do it with a friend! You know we don't always need to write alone. Children love to coauthor.

I'll write soon,

Nina

Nina

P.S.   I am including a writing process checklist I developed. You needn't treat it like a recipe, but maybe it will help you remember some of the elements we've talked about:

Writing Process Checklist

_____ Children choose their own topics.

_____ Children receive sustained and consistent time for daily writing process.

_____ Children keep a separate folder or notebook just for their drafts.

_____ Children have daily access to the sharing sign-up sheet for full class sharing.

_____ Children share their work in all stages of the process (draft through publication).

_____ Children use T—Tell what you like, A—Ask questions and G—Give ideas (TAG) during full-class sharing.

_____ Children self-edit and also edit the drafts of their peers.

_____ Children have daily access to book covers and publishing paper to publish their individual stories.

_____ Children put their published books in individual boxes or in the classroom library for their peers to read during reading process.

_____ The teacher writes and shares her work at least once a week to model the importance of writing.

_____ The teacher conducts five-minute skills lessons to the full class within the context of a child's writing and during the appropriate stage of the process (for example, handwriting is spoken about during writing of the final copy).

_____ The teacher edits drafts together with the child after that child has self-edited and has had a peer edit the draft.

_____ The teacher keeps a log to note each individual child's progress.

_____ The teacher encourages children's co-authorship.

_____ The teacher makes sure that book covers, the sign-up sheet, publishing paper and an audience are always available to the children.

LETTER #6
TEACHING AS HUMAN COMMUNITY:
RETHINKING THE BLUEBIRDS,
ROBINS AND BUZZARDS

> *The student is the subject of the process of learning to read and write as an act of knowing and creating. The fact that he or she needs the teacher's help, as in any pedagogical situation, does not mean that the teacher's help nullifies the student's creativity and responsibility for constructing his or her own written language and for reading this language. . . . [T]he teacher cannot put it together for the student; that is the student's creative task. . . . Words should be laden with the meaning of the people's existential experience, and not of the teacher's experience.*
>
> *(Freire and Macedo, 1987, pp. 34-35).*

Dear Students,

Hi! You may have wondered how in the world you can teach all thirty children in your classroom to read. They are all so different and all of them have different needs. I suppose that some of you think back occasionally on your own experiences in school and particularly that one experience so many of us have in common: the reading group. Do you remember what group they placed you in? How did it feel? Was this a positive experience? Why? or why not?

I guess I'm one of the lucky ones. I can only vaguely remember my reading group. I do remember the "Dick and Jane" readers and how incredibly boring they were. I remember I loved to read. It was my saving grace in school since I was horrible in math. I remember I was once bitten by my dog (yes, my dog!) and had to stay home the week before Christmas. My teacher brought me a book—I still can see it in my mind: *365 Bedtime Stories.* Its paper was like newspaper print with two or three stories to each page. I can still see the black line between the stories. I cherished this book. I read over and over again the names of my classmates who signed it. I don't remember the teacher's name but I do remember her face and her short brown hair.

Now as I write this I remember she was the same teacher who told us that John F. Kennedy had been shot. It must have been when I was in second grade. We stood for a moment of silence and I remember the wooden desk I was sitting in, on the right side of the room, in the row next to the blackboard, under the clock. I remember her telling us about the President. Then she ran out of the room, crying.

I remember a teacher named Mrs. Civetello. She had medium-length blonde hair (not really bright blonde, more mixed with brown) and must have used hair spray. I remember her because once she gave me one of her books. Inside the front cover she had printed "C. Civetello." I remember looking at the initial and wondering what her first name was: Carol? Carolyn? Catherine? I don't recall the book's content at all. Just the cover (hard, greenish-gray like khaki) and my teacher's name and that feeling of importance because my teacher had given me one of her books.

Then there was the time in sixth grade when my marks in reading suddenly plummeted. No one knew why because I scored high on a reading level test. (I remember the little piece of yellow paper on which my teacher wrote "11.5" and said, "Give this to your parents. You are reading at an 11th grade level.") They called my father to discuss the problem. (I remember because my father didn't live with us and he had to make a special trip from Brooklyn to Queens.) They finally realized I needed glasses. I had been too embarrassed to tell them. My teacher started writing her fill-in-the blanks reading tests on the board and I couldn't see them. She moved me from the back of the room to the front, but I was too embarrassed to tell her I still couldn't see. So every Friday I handed in blank pieces of paper. She was an elderly teacher with white short hair and wire glasses. I remember her, too, because she taught us about Brazil and she said that every summer she went to Rio de Janeiro. She was the one who handed me that yellow piece of paper saying I was such an accomplished reader. I finally got glasses so that I could see again.

My most vivid memories are from third grade. A young teacher named Miss Teasel crushed my self-esteem on two different occasions. First came an audition for the class play "Oliver." Since I was blonde and blue-eyed, like the kid in the play, I was told to sing anything I knew in front of the class. I picked "The Star-Spangled Banner." I bombed, terribly. I lost the part, and everyone knew why. I don't sing well, and to this day I cannot sing in front of people.

The second embarrassment had to do with reading worksheets. We were required to work through a reading workbook every day. I hated this book. I refused to do it. I wrote yes and no randomly for every question in the book. Did I ever get into trouble! Miss Teasel went ballistic. She called in my parents, I got a beating, and was forced to do the workbook. Success? No. Relief? Yeah. When the last day of school came and the bell rang. That was my third grade success. (MS)

I began playing with a toy and all of a sudden it broke. I mean I didn't do it on purpose. Then all of a sudden one of the kids told the teacher what happened. Ms. Buckholt slammed the door shut and began hollering at us and at me especially. She threw my desk outside and told me to get out. I'll never forget how much I cried that day. I had never been so embarrassed in my whole life. I was such a quiet child, and that day I became even quieter. (DT)

When I was in third grade, I made it to the spelling bee. I'd always made it into the top five since first grade. In my third grade year, I was left with only one more person, a boy. I was so excited and nervous. This was the first time a boy had made it to the finals, and when he was up he got two chances to respond. On his second try he got it correct. When it was my turn, I got one chance and I misspelled the word. But I figured it was okay; I was going to get a second try. But I wasn't. I was told, "Sorry, good try!" This was in front of the entire school. No one said anything. (JT)

I will never forget the third grade. I went to school in Miami Lakes and I really liked this grade. We read a lot of poems and drew a lot of maps. One day, a new boy came to our class. He was from Greece and spoke no English. I remember feeling sensitive to his awkwardness, as the teacher sat him right next to her desk in front of the class. I knew he needed a friend. When lunch came, I went to him and communicated in a kind of sign language. We sat together. I tried teaching him new words like "lunch," "food," "cafeteria,"and "teacher." We both giggled. It was real nice for both of us. Years passed, but Jani and I always remembered each other. We both went to the same junior high and high school. I'll never forget our conversation one day after we graduated from high school. We both remembered that day in third grade when we bonded. (LA)

Mrs. Murdock was the type of teacher who would humiliate students in front of the entire class. Also, she discussed you with the other teachers if she didn't like you. I remember one day she called on me to answer a question, and I tried to answer the question in broken English. She made fun of me in front of the entire class. I can still remember her disgusting and smart remarks. I remember her pointing at me and saying, "You refugee, you will never make it in this country. All you will do is pump gas." I remember my eyes began to water and I felt the size of an ant. (HF)

I was in the third grade. We were not allowed to talk. We were just supposed to sit quietly and do our board work. Well, I asked my friend a question and the teacher got upset with me for talking in class. She gave me a pink slip and told me to go to the office. I was petrified. I cried and begged the teacher to give me another chance. She did. I'll never forget that. I think that is the reason I really don't talk much in class. (LG)

I remember the fifth-grade class in which I was first introduced to journal writing. The teacher and I had a connection that year that developed into a real friendship. I think that this also developed a habit that has lasted to this day. This opportunity to communicate with the teacher through my journals gave writing a new, important meaning. I still have the worn-out old journal and I looked back on it before I wrote this paper. It was filled with questions, answers, and most importantly, enthusiasm. (LF)

I remember when I was in sixth grade. The teacher began to notice that I was just a little bit hyper and disruptive when I got my work (seatwork, of course) done. Constantly, I was in the office and the teacher would call my mother. The teacher wanted to label me an "emotionally handicapped child who could not control her behavior." I was referred to the school psychologist and she decided to give me an IQ test. I got a score of 130. My teacher then would give me "additional work," and I was given a higher level reading book all to myself. I hated it! I was all alone and I had no one to talk to about the stories I read. I also had to do a lot of the things alone. Everyday I would cry, but the teacher would just tell me that I was different and things would get better. (AR)

When I came to this country from Cuba I was put back a year. In my country, at four years of age, I was writing cursive script and knew how to read. But in this school system they didn't care what level you're in, if you don't know the language you fall behind. When second grade came along—I'll never forget my teacher's name—Mrs. Thorne wanted to put me back a year because I wasn't reading as fast as she wanted me to. She told my parents I had to be put back a year, but my parents disagreed because they knew I was capable of learning and I was smart enough to challenge the tasks that this teacher gave me. I will never forget what a bad experience I had in second grade. It has never been erased from my mind—that old lady's face. (SM)

In the sixth grade I was very shy and never spoke in front of class unless I had to. I was terrified that I would give the wrong answer or say something stupid and look like a fool. One day, another student was scratching his nails on the chalkboard and it was driving me crazy. The teacher told the boy to cut it out because that noise made her sick. I felt the same way, and I gathered up all my courage and managed to say "me too." The teacher looked at me in shock and said to everyone, "Oh, my goodness! Did you all hear that squeaky little voice over there?" Then she began to repeat it in a tiny voice, "Me, too. Me too." I felt devastated. All the courage I had drawn up to try and join in and be a part of the class, she just shot down." (CM)

I remember the day I began to hate coming to school: I'm in fourth grade and it's my first day in this class. My teacher, Mrs. Starling, waits for us at the door. As I approach, I notice she is holding her finger closing her lips shut. I guess she wants us to be quiet. She looks awfully scary. Her eyebrows close together, makes her look mean and angry. She doesn't smile much. I guess she wants us to be scared. (IP)

The most vivid memory of my early school years is when I was in preschool. I was a very finicky child. For breakfast I had to have my chocolate milk warm. Everyone else had to drink it cold and white. Every day the lunch lady would do me the favor. Then one day the teacher caught me in her kitchen. She was appalled and sent me to the principal. The moment I walked in the door, I saw it there on her desk—a carton of white milk. Yuck! I knew what was to follow: a force feeding of the milk. First she tried to tell me that it was good. I knew it tasted horrible. She tried to get me to have a small sip. I almost threw up. Finally, she grew so frustrated with me that she held my nose, pulled my head back and tried to force the milk down my throat. The fight was on. I was quite a stubborn little four-year-old. What ensued was a terrible struggle. My hair was pulled; milk was spilled on me and her; my arms were pinned down and my cheeks pressed to drink. The principal's arms were scratched and her face was red. Finally, somehow, my mother got there and was shocked at what she saw. There I was, covered in milk, my face filled with tears, my hair all over the place, being held down by the principal with a milk carton in her hand and just as disheveled. Needless to say, I never went back there again and I will NEVER drink white milk. Yuck! (AP)

The clearest memory I have of a teacher is my seventh-grade teacher, Sister Mary Joseph. Seventh grade was a tough year. My best friend, Terri, was sick with cancer. All that school year Sister took me to the hospital for visits. She took me aside and talked with me whenever I felt the need. She's a huge woman and gave great hugs!

On April 6, 1981, Terri died. I had not been notified as it happened late at night. I arrived at school to a teary Sister. She had grouped all the seventh graders in one room and told us the terrible news. Of course, I was shocked. She felt awful—she thought I already knew. She again took me aside and helped me through it. Sister sang at the funeral and was there for me every step of the way.

Just last year she was there for me again. My dad passed away and she helped us to plan the funeral. Sister Mary Joseph has a heart of gold, and I will never forget her. (CK)

When I was in fourth grade I had a friend who became my shadow. Wherever I went she followed. I often showed off and pretended to know absolutely everything about life. One morning, our teacher told us that a week from that day we would be going on a treasure hunting field trip to the Sierra mountains west of Madrid, Spain. Our teacher wrote on the board a key with symbols, that would help us in our treasure hunt. The day of the field trip I wore a red sweater, which I wasn't supposed to wear because Señorita Rosa told us we might see a bull. Well, I thought I knew everything. Everyone started the treasure hunt, including us. First left, then right, then fifty steps diagonally to the right. Soon we were lost. I thought it was no big deal that Elena and I had some difference in our symbols because I just figured mine were right. The more I showed confidence in front of Elena, the higher we climbed and soon we were both crying. We stopped to rest for awhile. All of a sudden, I saw Elena turning white, and I followed her eyes to see where they were looking. When I looked, I froze. I have never been so scared in my entire life. There were three bulls taking a nap, and here I was with my red sweater, thinking of Señorita Rosa and how I would never be able to tell her she was right because I was going to be killed. Two hours or so passed and we started hearing our teachers' voices. I had never seen a teacher as a hero, and that day, I sure did. During our two hours together, Elena and I were basically statues, waiting for just a slight movement from a bull. Thanks to our heroes we were saved.

Two years ago I went back to Spain to visit my old friends. When I saw Elena I was wearing a red blazer and as soon as she saw me, she burst into laughter. When she told me why she was laughing and reminded me about the bulls, I joined in. When she asked me what my major was and I told her "education" she said, "Vas a ser un heroe?" (You're going to be a hero?) I said, "I hope so." (JT)

I hope you noticed that my own memory of "reading instruction" as well as the memories of my university students all involve human relationships. As you can see, too, most of these school memories do not center on what we remember or learned academically. We remember the feelings and the people involved more than "the material." From stories like these, you could easily conclude that the particular books we read were less important than with whom we read them and how we felt when we read them. Indeed, to talk about reading as separate from the social context of the classroom is to interrupt a connection to human relationships. Reading is connecting to a message and creating personal meaning.

Personal meaning extends beyond the text itself and is created within the context of past, present and future thoughts and feelings. Meaning depends on many influences—time, place, text, with whom connections are being made. I'm sure you've experienced reading this way. Have you ever read the same book or article at different times and found totally different meanings each time? Have you ever seen a movie with a friend and the two of you left with completely different impressions of it? This happens to me a lot!

Have you ever gone back to read an old paper you've written, perhaps to revise it for another class, and find yourself surprised that you even wrote it? This happens to me often, and I am amazed at how different I sounded in the past. "I can't believe I wrote this!" I say to myself. Either the piece reads so powerfully that I feel renewed pride or it argues a position I no longer believe and find naive. When you think about it, then, how can reading ever be a static activity? Reading is language itself and language is inherently human and dynamic. How exciting that print engraved on the page continues to change and grow! Maybe that's why I love to read so much. Reading is entering into a relationship with yourself, with the author and with people in your past, present and future. Yes, future too. Look at the literacy experiences my university students described. Do you think these experiences influenced them and their future plans? Indeed they did; in fact, powerfully negative or positive encounters directly influenced their decisions to enter education. How have your reading experiences in school influenced your decision to enter the field of education?

As you have begun to sense, "reading" is a broad and inclusive term that encompasses a particular text while encircling all of life. As I tell my university students, language arts is life. I don't say this facetiously. Language is what makes us human. It surrounds us totally and is as dynamic and passionate as we ourselves are. Whatever we do in our classrooms we must make sure that we do not drain the life out of language arts. We must ensure that all our children continue to live life fully in our literacy programs. What can you do to make certain the passion of life lives in your literacy work? I can tell you what I do: I read. I write. And I love it! My passion for literacy permeates all I do, and when this enthusiasm touches the souls of my students, they begin to eat, drink, sleep and live language arts. Do you read for enjoyment—pure enjoyment? If not, start now as you work on developing your love for reading. When you begin to read for yourself, you will begin to love it. This love will be a light, guiding your students on their quest for personal meaning and growth.

Most of you are familiar with the conventional way we teach reading in our schools—with the three reading groups. We usually find the "highest" reading group (closest to heaven) named after a beloved animal or bird, like the Bluebird. The middle reading group is named after a more prosaic bird like the Robin (which, being heavier, has to try harder to fly toward heaven). The "lowest" group is most always named after an ugly bird like the Buzzard (with no hope of redemption). So begins the catechism of conventional reading instruction. The teachings remain powerful, sending clear messages about success and failure, hope and despair.

When we group readers this way we label and limit the definition of "reading"—reading becomes "the book" for "your group." We label and limit types of reading material—"only the Bluebirds can read that." We label and limit our questioning strategies,—"these questions are too complicated for the Buzzards." And we label and limit relationships—"yes, James and Michael have been friends since first grade and they've always been in the highest reading group!"

The Buzzards are the Buzzards and the Bluebirds are the Bluebirds and most times the groups never mix. Children tend to remain in these ability groups and certain relationships as a consequence form with other students in their group, with students outside the group, and with the teacher. When we group according to "reading ability" we limit other characteristics of our students. We limit their opportunities to express their personal strengths and gifts. We also limit our personal view of them. When we limit reading material because we feel some students can't handle it, we limit the whole child, his or her relationships, and his or her personal view. We actually teach children to limit themselves.

Before we discuss about how reading happens in my room (and notice I avoided the term "reading instruction" which fails to include all that I think reading is), let's discuss the philosophy that underlies the grouping of children into high, middle and low reading groups. What do you think teachers believe about language arts instruction when they group this way? What does this type of grouping say about their view of literacy?

When we group in levels, we tend to believe that reading proceeds in a hierarchical way. That is, first you need to know this, then you can learn that. This view is also called the "readiness view" of literacy. Therefore, children placed with the Buzzards cannot move up to Bluebirds or Robins until they master "Buzzard skills" and, of course Bluebirds and Robins need never move down to the Buzzards since they have already mastered the "low-level" skills. This skills-oriented view breaks reading apart into pieces in order to "make it easier" and "more manageable" for the child. When children can manage more and more "pieces," they get closer and closer to being "ready to read."

Let's pause to think about why teachers might do this. Are they, in fact, more concerned with themselves as "controllers" or "managers" than with what is best for their students? Why do you think this type of piecemeal instruction might seem easier to handle for a teacher? What type of activities might take place in the readiness classroom? What type of materials might be available there? What type of interactions might occur in the different reading groups? Would the teacher be speaking to the children in the same way? Would the teacher be asking the same questions in the different reading groups? What do you think the children might be doing when the teacher meets with other reading groups?

A Reading Readiness Program

Materials in a reading readiness classroom would include
- basals (leveled books with controlled vocabulary-teacher editions),
- workbooks for each reading group, and
- extra worksheets for students who finish their workbook or boardwork before the teacher finishes with other reading groups.

Some teachers find such instruction easier to handle because of the teacher editions that include step-by-step scripts and leveled books and worksheets.

Children who are not involved with the teacher in a reading group generally fill in worksheets or copy work from the board. Teachers in the readiness room believe that students cannot read unless they receive direct instruction from the teacher.

In a readiness classroom that groups according to "reading level" different interactions occur in different groups. Teachers talk to the Bluebirds in a different way than to the Buzzards. Bluebirds hear such higher-level questions as "Why do you think the character felt like that?" "How would you feel if this happened to you?" The Buzzards hear such low-level questions as "What color dress was the girl wearing?" "How old is the girl's brother?"

Bluebird Questions

1. What do you think the father will do when he comes home? Why?
2. Do you think her brother was upset with her? Why? Why not?
3. How would you feel if you were the brother? Why?
4. How would you have written this story differently?
5. Do you think the author really had an experience like this when she was younger?

Robin Questions

1. Why do you think the girl acted that way?
2. What would you have done if you were that girl?
3. Do you think the mother was happy when she heard what happened?
4. What do you think the girl will say to her brother?
5. Did you like this story? Why? Why not?

Buzzard Questions

1. What happened first?
2. What happened second?
3. What happened third?
4. What did the mother say?
5. How old was the girl's brother?

After reading these typical questions for each group, who do you think is being engaged in the most purposeful conversation? Is it fair that only the higher levels have interesting conversations about their reading? Why would anyone want to deprive some students of such conversations? Unfortunately, that is what reading-level grouping does. The Buzzards experience the most boring, controlled vocabulary and conversation while the Bluebirds and sometimes the Robins experience more interesting work.   Is this division really necessary? Those who come from the readiness perspective believe it is. They believe that children need to be "readied" with low-level questions before they can answer higher-level questions. Remember we talked about education being a mirror of society? How does this description of reading groups mirror and maintain our larger society? Think about it. How are lives determined by economic class? What does our society value most in its people? What happens if people in our society don't "measure up" to the established images (like beauty, intelligence and wealth)?

What do you believe? In their natural conversations, what do young children speak about? Do they talk only about concrete details? Do they talk about feelings, friendships and their own lives? How can we change the lower-ordered questions to make them more real?

Let's try. "How old was the girl's brother?" Let's change this low-level question so it has more personal meaning for a student? What about "Do you have a brother?" "How old is he?" "How does it feel being a younger or older brother?" "Do you think the girl in the story felt this way too?"

Why do only the Bluebirds get to answer these "higher-level" questions? Can't all children answer them? Of course, they can. When we open our questions so that all children can relate personally and authentically to the reading at hand, the reading process takes on a dimension unavailable with the readiness view.   It's a view that sees reading as relationship, a natural aspect of communication that needs to be purposeful and authentic for the reader. It's a view that sees all students as communicators trying to make personal sense of the world.

When we see students this way, we broaden the definition of literacy to include "making sense" and, therefore, recognize it as already part of the child's repertoire. When the definition includes "making sense," students already come to school as literate beings. My job as an educator is to maintain an environment that encourages the children's literacy to emerge within the classroom community.

This perspective is sometimes called the "emergent literacy" perspective, and it is based on philosophical tenets quite different from those that guide the readiness perspective. I prefer to call it "authentic literacy" or "critical literacy," since what we're talking about here addresses cultural and political issues within the context of literacy. What do you think are the major differences? How would these differences influence reading activities, conversations and groupings?

Critical Literacy

Children are viewed as the major "resource" in the classroom community, therefore, the classroom "materials" would include
- student writing and choice of reading, whether written in dominant language or not;
- student experiences, reflections, and questions as the basis of all discussions as the teacher facilitates growth;
- books covering many themes and interests in the dominant language as well as the first languages of the children;
- personal diaries, reading reflection logs, student checklists, goal sheets and. portfolios;
- publishing material for students to publish their own work for community   reading;
- flexible discussion groups chosen by students as they discuss their reading and writing material;
- authentic questions posed by both teacher and students;
- outside community visitors to the classroom community to engage in and enrich discussions;
- interactions that help students help their classmates as well as receive help (for example, helping each other maintain the rules of community and lending personal suggestions or expertise to projects); and
- full responsibility and participation in the community.

Reading from a readiness perspective, then, is predicated on a hierarchical group of skills that, when assembled, creates reading. Reading from an emergent perspective, by contrast, considers reading as communication that occurs within authentic communication contexts. Authentic communication is whole communication that makes no sense when broken up into smaller parts. In fact, Vygotsky discussed this breaking apart of literacy as analogous to the breaking apart of water (H_2O) into its individual elements: "When one approaches the problem of thinking and speech by decomposing it into its elements, one adopts the strategy of the man who resorts to the decomposition of water into hydrogen and oxygen in his search for a scientific explanation of the characteristics of water, its capacity to extinguish fire. . . . This man will discover, to his chagrin, that hydrogen burns and oxygen sustains combustion. He will never succeed in explaining the characteristics of the whole by analyzing the characteristics of its elements" (qtd. in Moll, 1990, p. 6).

I am a teacher who believes in children's needs and desires to communicate and make sense of the world. This belief influences my definition of literacy, the way I maintain my classroom environment and the conversations in which I encourage all children to participate. While my philosophy of literacy supports this view of emergence, it also includes political aspects less clearly addressed in the emergent literacy perspective. I believe that children come to me as purposeful communicators who need and want to be seen as such. Accordingly, our conversations are real and personal. Whether we speak about a wordless book or a book with many chapters, I try to connect all conversation to the child's own personal story and experiences. This strengthening of each individual voice is crucial in the transformation of our society into a more just society. Traditionally the higher reading groups are the only children with a chance to strengthen their voices because of the more authentic questions and conversations they negotiate. But in my classroom, all children have the right to express who they are and to be asked important questions that make sense. I would avoid asking "What color is the girl's dress?" in isolation. But I might ask it of a child who likes red or happens herself to be wearing a red dress. (This is stretching it, though, because I would wonder how important the whole issue of dress color is anyway.) If I were forced for some reason to ask questions about the color of a dress, I would try to do it in the most meaningful way possible: "Why do you think the author had the girl wear this red dress?" "If you were the author what color dress would you have the girl wear? Why?"

What questions would you ask your students? How can you enlarge your questioning so that all your students hear meaningful, purposeful questions? Would you be the only one questioning your students? How could you set up your literacy environment so that students could question each other? Why might it be constructive for students to question each other?

I think we need to rethink the whole idea of "reading levels." It's incredible how this one concept has driven our traditional views of literacy. Indeed, the idea of "levels of reading" has helped perpetuate a remarkably narrow view of literacy. Do you ever wonder who decided on these levels? What textbook company have we allowed to shape our reading curriculum? Why do we assume that levels remain static? Could they not be a function of type of material, reader interest, reader motivation, emotional state or context? Think about it. What do you have a hard time reading? I know I have an incredibly difficult time reading instructional material, like how to record on a VCR. Forget about a sewing pattern; I don't even know where to begin!

What do you think? How does the concept of levels support the principles of reading groups? How, in turn, does it reinforce the economic, political and social structures of our society? Think about it. Our economic structure is based on how many levels? That's right: upper, middle and lower.

Because I see myself as a social change agent in my classroom, I believe that what I do there will either maintain the structures of our society or transform them. I believe that our society needs to be transformed into a more just society where all people are valued and receive respect for their uniqueness. Our society needs to be transformed into one where we welcome difference and consider it a strength. The notion that we should all reach "one standard of perfection" needs to be examined so that we can stop the senseless competition that derives from comparing one person to another. When we are valued for the human beings we are, we become less threatened by others, we feel safe, then we feel successful and accepted. This acceptance and safety helps us to value ourselves. In turn, we begin to feel more comfortable valuing others around us.

I view literacy, therefore, as the vehicle to likely promote transformative or emancipatory education. Freire put it this way: "The notion that literacy is a matter of learning the standard language still informs the vast majority of literacy programs and manifests its logic in the renewed emphasis on technical reading and writing skills. [But] literacy cannot be viewed as simply the development of skills aimed at acquiring the dominant standard language. This view sustains a notion of ideology that systematically negates rather than makes meaningful cultural experiences. . . .Literacy must be viewed as an integral part of the way in which people produce, transform, and reproduce meaning. Literacy must be seen as a medium that constitutes and affirms the historical and existential moments of lived experience" (Freire and Macedo, 1987).

When we talk about these perceptions of literacy within a historical and political context, many of my students express hopelessness, despair and a feeling of being overwhelmed. "It's so much to think about! There are so many problems! We can't do everything! All the responsibility is on teachers!" While it is normal at times to feel overwhelmed, as reflective teachers we must overcome feelings that block action and decide what we can do. My favorite line is "Pick your battle." That is, while you can't fight or change everything at once, you can decide what you want to do at particular times. One year you might decide to concentrate on giving all your students a choice of reading material. Another year you may decide to fight another "battle." Remember, that while you might not change everything around you, whatever you do (or don't do) as a teacher makes a powerful statement.

Over my years of teaching, I have chosen to maintain my classroom to resemble the way I wish society were. Because I believe that competition spawns insecure and threatened people and unjust structures, I try to eliminate competition in my room. One child's success does not depend on another child's failure. I value all children for who they are; and while, of course, they all progress, they do not have to progress at the same rate as the child sitting next to them progresses. Indeed, consider how ridiculous the notion of comparison really is. How could we even think that two children could learn at the same speed, absorb information the same way, enjoy the same things? Why would we want such uniformity? We are all complex human beings and to think that we can or have the right to control another person's complexity is ludicrous. At least that's what I think. What do you think?

To ensure that the reading process remains purposeful for my students, the element of choice is always present. It is not just my responsibility to determine "purpose" but the students' responsibility as well. When you think about it, who better to decide what is purposeful than the students themselves? After all, what is meaningful to one student might not be meaningful to another. Therefore, the children in my classroom choose the material they want to read. What do you think such children would choose? Why? How do you think choice or lack of it would influence your behavior and attitude toward reading?

The reading that goes on in my classroom is both varied and structured at the same time. Reading involves a number of activities that include silent reading, team reading and sharing. Children choose what they want to read for silent reading, then take it to team reading to discuss with their peers. Books available include children's literature at all levels and in all genres as well as the books published by the students themselves, placed alongside such other authors as Judy Blume, Beverly Cleary, Dr. Seuss, Roald Dahl.

While children choose their own literacy material, they also are part of a literacy community and need, therefore, to follow certain guidelines. Also because they are part of a community, it is part of their responsibility to help both themselves and other community members remain successful. Therefore, guidelines for activities are agreed upon, written down and displayed in the classroom during the first week of school.

Silent Reading Rules

1. We read silently.
2. We remain in our seats.
3. We have our own books.
4. We only read during silent reading.
5. Children and adults all read at the same time.

Team Reading Rules

1. We take the book(s) we were reading during silent reading.
2. Two, three or four people make up a team.
3. All teams are mixed (each team needs to have boys and girls).
4. We talk about reading and other subjects connected to what we're reading.
5. We help our friends form our teams.

Some Questions to Ask During Team Reading

Do you like your book? Why or why not?
Who is your favorite character? Why?
What's your favorite part of the book and why?
Why did you choose this book?
What other books has this author written?
Why do you think the author wrote this book?
Where do you think the author got his or her ideas?
What is the problem of the story?
What is the solution of the story?
Where does the story take place?
What genre is your story?
Where do you think the author got the topic?
Which character would you like to be? Why?
How would you feel if that were your problem?
If you were the author, what would you change? Why?
What was the best event that happened?
What was the worst event that happened?
Would you keep the same title or change it? Why?
What part of the story connects to the title?
How would the character's life change if the story were set in a different time?
How would the characters be different if the story were set in another country?
What ideas would you use from the book to write your own story? Why?
How will this book change your life? Why?

A familiar question from those more comfortable with the conventional three reading group room is how does one teacher keep up with what all the children are reading. It seems like a lot of reading! Your answer to this question would depend on what you believe your job as a teacher is. If you believe that a good teacher must know exactly what each child is doing or saying or thinking every minute of the day and must be the only person who questions and intervenes with every child, this type of structure would be difficult for you to handle. If, on the other hand, you trust that children in a safe, non-competitive room who are allowed a choice of literacy material can help guide purposeful literacy discussions, this type of reading community will appeal to you.

Let's examine the rationale that forms the foundation of this type of community. When I make decisions about what type of activities and interactions to encourage, I try to connect them to purposeful, meaningful interactions that occur "on the outside." When you think about real reading behavior—that is, what adults who love to read do when it comes to literacy—what type of interactions come to your mind? What do you do or say or think when you've just finished a really good book? Do you try to remember the color of the dress the heroine wore? Would you tell a friend about the dress or would you talk about more personal connections? Would you suggest that he or she read it?

When I read a really good book (or see a really good movie) I want to discuss my experience of it with my friends and hope that they share my experience. I'd talk about the powerful imagery, the events that I identified with personally, other books I have read by this author, or other books I want to read. This kind of interaction is, for me, real reading. Because I believe this about reading, I am obligated to offer this to my students as well. Why would we force children into contrived and stilted interactions we call reading but really have nothing to do with reading at all?

Do you ever ask a friend what reading level he or she has reached? Or do you ask, "What book are you reading?" If you were allowed to develop a love for reading, you will ideally be interested enough to ask what others are reading. Traditionally, though, we failed to encourage a love for reading because we actually discouraged children from reading! When children fill out worksheets, fill in the blanks, match initial consonants, sit in a group where everyone completes the same worksheet, they are not reading.

My elementary school children read by reading and talking about their personal books of choice. So every day all children (and I) have an opportunity for sustained silent reading. It lasts for about 15 or 20 minutes, unless of course I'm on a really good chapter and need to extend silent reading time so I can finish it (Remember we talked about how a teacher's personal love of reading influences her students, and sometimes I illustrate my love of reading). I might even say to the class, "Oh, I know silent reading is supposed to be over, but can we please have another five minutes? I really want to finish my chapter!" The students, of course, say "yes" because they love to read, too.

Anyway, after silent reading the children break up into teams to discuss their books. This is a natural next step, don't you think? As we said earlier, most of us want to talk to a friend about a book or movie we absolutely love. So do the children, particularly when they read books they have chosen themselves. Our team reading groups are flexible, and generally the children choose their teams. If I see the same children forming a team over a long period, I might say to them, "Tomorrow you need to find other people for your teams. This way you will have a chance to learn from everyone." The next day, I will, of course, make sure to hold them accountable for following this directive. Also, if I see that someone is reading a book that might be of particular interest to another child, I will make sure to pass this information along:

> Nina: I see, Alba, you are reading about horses. You know Maria loves horses too. Maybe you can do team reading with her today.

After silent reading I generally direct them into team reading this way:

> Nina: Okay, let's get into team reading. Remember the rules and make sure you are not too close to another team.

The children then find their team members and a place to begin their discussions. Usually they find a place on the floor. A few choose to stay sitting at their desks. Why do you think? I suspect that most like to leave their desks by this time since they have been seated at their desks for twenty minutes during silent reading. If it is the beginning of the year or if we have visitors in the room, I will review the rules this way:

Nina:	How many people make up a team?
Lonny:	Two.
Nina:	Good. Does there have to be only two in a team?
Graham:	No, there can be three or four.
Nina:	That's right. In this classroom a team can be either two, three or four. Why aren't there five in a team?
Laura:	Because with five there might not be enough time for everyone to share.
Nina:	That's right. We want to make sure that we all get a chance to discuss at least a little bit about our books. Is there ever one person in a team?
Franny:	No.
Nina:	Why not?
Kelly:	That's not a team because there is no one else to talk to.
Nina:	That's true. Now what will you do if you see someone is not in a team and is wandering around alone?
Brenda:	Help them find a team.
Nina:	Good. Remember one of our rules is to help each other form our teams. Also, remember we do not always have to be with the same people. We can discuss our books with different people each day. Why is that important?
Desiree:	So that we learn from everybody.
Nina:	Yes, also remember that all teams are mixed. Why do we make sure of this?
Steve:	So that we learn that both girls and boys have good things to say.
Nina:	Exactly. We need to make sure we include all people in our groups. Now what happens if you have a group of only boys?
Char:	You have to go to another group and find a girl to come in.
Nina:	That's right and girls if someone needs you for their group you need to go cheerfully since it is part of our job to help our friends with forming the teams.
Dave:	Okay, let's get into team reading now and remember if you run out of things to discuss, look at the chart of questions we wrote. I'll be around to listen to your conversations.

While the children are in the groups I circulate among to the teams to facilitate their discussions. While I often leave the types of discussions up to the children, at times I am more directive. For example, if during writers' workshop we had a discussion about character traits, I usually carry this discussion over to silent reading and team reading:

Nina:	Before we go into silent reading, let's talk a little about character traits. Remember the character in Aurora's story? Who can tell me a little bit about her?
Barry:	She was very mean and scary.
Nina:	Aurora, is that true?
Aurora:	Yes, she was.
Nina:	Okay. What else about this character?
Cathy:	She was also rough and gruff.
Nina:	Good. All those were examples of character traits. Now what I want you to do as you are silently reading is think about the traits the characters you are reading about have. Then discuss some of them in team reading. Okay. Let's all go into silent reading.

In this instant after silent reading is over and before we transition into team reading, I talk to the class as a whole again and remind them about the first topic of discussion:

Nina:	Okay, before you go into team reading, raise your hand to tell us a few of the character traits that you found in your reading.
Paul:	Shy.
Nina:	Good. How do you know your character was shy?
Marty:	Well, when Mr. Murphy talked to her she didn't answer and the author said she trembled.
Nina:	Good! That really supports the opinion that your character is shy? Someone else?

I'll ask two or three more students and then reinforce the assignment with these questions:

Nina:	Now when you go into team reading what is the first thing you will talk about?
Susie:	Character traits.
Nina:	That's right, and make sure that everyone has a chance to talk. What happens if everyone talks and you still are in team reading? What will you talk about next?
Becky:	We could look on the question chart and use some of those.
Nina:	Good. Let's get into team reading.

Most times, before returning the children to their individual desks, I begin to close team reading this way:

Nina:	Let's come together as a class for a minute (the children don't move, they stay in their teams). We have five more minutes for team reading. What we're going to do at the end is go to

each team and ask for two or three character traits your team discussed. Okay, start deciding on what traits you want to share with the class and who will do the talking for your team.

After five minutes;

> Nina: Okay, let's come together and hear about your traits. Juan's team.

I pick the names randomly. We have no team leaders, and the children decide who will talk. I might notice that Henry hasn't talked for awhile and invite him to participate.

> Henry, why don't you tell us what you all discussed in your team?

The assigned homework always connects closely with the classroom conversations. Therefore, at the end of team reading I often ask the children to formulate some appropriate homework:

> Nina: So what do you think we should have for homework?
> Warren: Something to do with character traits.
> Nina: Yeah, that's what I was thinking, since we were just talking about them during team reading and during writing process. So any ideas?
> Eileen: We could write down the character traits of someone we wrote about.
> Nina: So maybe pick one of our own drafts or publications and talk about one of our characters. Someone else?
> Tatiana: We could pick a character from our personal reading book and list the traits.
> Nina: Good.
> Richard: We could write the character traits about ourselves or about our friend or someone in our family.
> Nina: Excellent ideas! Since all these ideas are so good, how about you each decide which one you want to do. Your homework can be to pick someone, either from your book or from your own writing or from your life or from anywhere and talk about their character traits.

You see here, I hope, what I do to facilitate a community where all the children are active, literate participants. I usually end these letters with questions for you to think about. This letter will be a little different and answer some general questions students frequently ask. I'll try not to answer these questions with more questions though I won't promise!

QUESTION:

What if children don't want to read during silent reading time? What if they don't even know how to read? How do you know they are even reading at this time?

ANSWER:

Just as during writing process I accept a wide variety of responses, during silent reading I also encourage the children to respond in their own personal ways. Therefore, while one child might flip through three books and another might stick with one book in five minutes time, they are *both* reading. Remember our discussion on definitions—with broad definitions we help all our children toward success. Therefore, just as I accept whatever they write as a valid and meaningful form of communication, whatever and how they choose to read is acceptable and valid. Because many children are unaccustomed to sustained periods of reading, some at first have difficulty understanding exactly what I expect. But this difficulty disappears quickly. First of all, the rules are designed with total student involvement and they are posted prominently in the classroom. When we begin silent reading, we do not allot an enormous amount of time. Just as in writing process, we slowly extend the silent reading time as the children become more comfortable with my expectations. The first week of sustained silent reading might last only five minutes or so. Much praise and recognition accompanies all appropriate behavior as we review and reinforce the rules. What also guarantees successful silent reading for all is my active participation. When the teacher reads her book every day and shows excitement about reading, she sends a clear message that this activity is extremely important and children want to be involved in important work. Remember, too, that because children choose their own reading material they probably *want* to read! What they are doing is meaningful, purposeful and personal, and so they become totally involved for a sustained period.

QUESTION:

I don't understand; how can children choose their own books? Even kindergartners?

ANSWER:

Believe it or not, as children become older they usually find it more difficult to accept the responsibility of choosing their own books, just as it is more difficult for them to choose their own topics. Most are so used to conventional reading instruction where the groups and stories are assigned that they are disconcerted when they are finally allowed to make these decisions. The kindergarten child, the young child, who has not yet been oppressed by convention usually accepts the responsibility of choice with enthusiasm and sheer joy! Don't you know what you like and don't like? Children know what they want to read, too. If they love animals they will look for animal books. If they love football they will look for books about football. Once children see that you support their choices, they jump headfirst into mountains of books, magazines, comics, catalogues and other reading material. What you need to do is provide this mountain. Get books, books, books—all levels, all kinds! Garage sales, discount stores, friends, families, libraries, the children themselves—use all these resources and more and your students will joyfully choose to read!

QUESTION:

What if children pick books that are too easy or too hard?

ANSWER:

I guess I'll have to answer this one with a question. What do you do when you pick a book that is too difficult for you? The answer for me would depend on why I started reading the book in the first place. If it is an instructional manual for a computer program I need to learn, I will probably struggle through it or find someone to help me since I need to use the program. If it is a book that is too difficult because the subject matter is incredibly dense or boring I would put it down. Moreover, I believe that when children have a chance to practice choosing, they choose appropriately for themselves. Appropriateness depends on many things: interest, time, likes, dislikes, and so on. Just as a child may want to see a movie more than a dozen times, it is also common to see a child reading the same book three, four or more times. My sister used to read her books ten times over. I said before, reading is not static; it is dynamic. Each reading is a different reading. Imagine the feeling of confidence and control children feel as they read a book for the third time. They know what is coming next, and they can see the images clearly. They become truly strong and confident. I will not deny this to my students. I trust that if they are reading a book for the third time they are reading it for a good reason, to meet a personal need. Nevertheless, I will encourage them to expand their choices. This is what I might say:

Nina: Jeff I see you have read that football book for three days in silent reading? Is it really good?

Jeff: Yes, it has a lot of pictures and my favorite player is Dan Marino.

Nina: Oh, so does it have pictures of Dan Marino?

Jeff: Yes.

Nina: So I guess you really like football. You know Javier reads a lot about football, too. I want you to talk to him during team reading so that tomorrow along with this book you can start reading another football book.

QUESTION:

What if all they read is comic books?

ANSWER:

Since I believe we all have a right to choose what we read, I have no problem with children consistently choosing comic books. I don't see comic books as a lesser form of literacy. Children who read comic books enjoy reading comic books and have a right not to feel inferior because they are not reading Shakespeare. How would you feel if someone saw you reading one of your favorite romance novels and said, "How could you read that? It's such trash!" I bet you would take this criticism personally—and you should. Attacking someone's choice of reading, writing and language is really touching on some personal issues about self. Therefore, we need to be sensitive in our responses to our students' choices. I would not tell a student that he or she could not read comic books during silent reading. What I do when I feel the student is ready to be pushed is suggest other books. I try, as well, to connect with the student's reading:

> Nina: I see, Chris, that you really love comic books. My son does, too. Do you collect them?
> Chris: Yes, I have about 10 collectibles!
> Nina: Wow, that's great! I used to collect Archie comics when I was little. What else do you like to do?
> Chris: I like to play with my dog.
> Nina: Oh! You know we have a lot of dog books in our library. For tomorrow when you get your silent reading material along with your comic books, I want you to include another book. Maybe you can pick one on dogs.

QUESTION:

Aren't there any common books that everyone in the class reads at the same time?

ANSWER:

Actually, there are but not because I think students need to read from the same books to read effectively. We read aloud from one book usually every day. It is a book the class chooses from student suggestions by voting. Either I or a student reads it. We read aloud because we love to read and it's fun. I find that many students end up wanting to read this book on their own, too. It becomes a hot commodity when they choose their reading material. You really know the children enjoy the book, too, when the school holds a book fair and the majority of children come in with that book. What happens in a natural way is that groups of children begin reading the same book. Amazing things do happen when you trust children's innate desire to communicate and grow!

QUESTION:

What if a child reads the same book over and over again?

ANSWER:

As we've already discussed, while it might appear we are reading the same material over and over again, each reading is, in fact, different. As things are, we do not give our students enough time to "read over" to reflect and connect. This time is critical for literacy growth and I avoid stifling it. I encourage the child to explore other pieces of literature along with the familiar piece but not in place of it:

> Nina: Wow, Alba, you must really love that book!! How many times have you read it so far?
> Alba: This is my fourth time. I do love it!
> Nina: Have you read any other books by Judy Blume?
> Alba: No. Just this one.
> Nina: You know we have *Tales of a Fourth Grade Nothing*. I think Eileen just finished it. Why don't you try that one? I bet you'll love it, too.

QUESTION:

What if they choose books that are below their level and how do you know what reading level everyone is on?

ANSWER:

As we've already discussed, this whole issue of levels is artificial in real literacy work. In a safe environment, children choose what they need. Actually, I find that children tend to choose more challenging books partly because of the prestige involved in being able to read difficult material. In a safe, respectful classroom, you'll see students feeling comfortable choosing books more traditionally seen as "kindergarten" books. I can almost guarantee you that a child who is allowed to choose will choose for a reason. Perhaps, the pictures are inviting, or the prose sounds like poetry, or the child has made a real personal connection with the topic. Some children might need or want to read books traditionally seen as inappropriate for their age,—for example, you might consider it useful for Frank to read *The Cat in the Hat*.

Frank is in fifth grade and his past literacy experiences have made him feel uncomfortable with books. What could you do to connect real purpose to reading this book? What I frequently do is allow students to practice reading aloud so that when they are ready, they can share with another class like a kindergarten or a first grade. A purposeful homework assignment in connection to this book might be "Read this story aloud to younger siblings and cousins and ask them what they liked about the book."

QUESTION:

How do you know if the children are progressing? How do you facilitate their reading growth?

ANSWER:

First of all, as I've said before, I never measure one child's progress against another's and try to eliminate such comparisons in my classroom community. I know a child is progressing in reading if he or she is reading every day and connecting to these readings. I can monitor these connections since they constantly emerge during full class sessions, team reading discussions and reading log entries. As you've seen in earlier dialogues, I facilitate growth through discussion and suggestions or directives ("Along with your comic book you need to read another form of literature"). I also facilitate growth as I model active involvement in all literacy work. Remember, though, that I am hardly the only one facilitating growth: The whole community—through discussions, sharing, reading and writing, facilitates each other's growth, including mine.

QUESTION:

How do you know if they're even talking about reading during team reading?

ANSWER:

You ask! It sounds simple and it is. Why don't more teachers ask their students what they want, like, need, and are doing? Yes, most people do, in fact, know what they need. When children have choice of reading material, they *want* to talk about it. We don't have to force them. If they seem not to be focused on the discussion at hand, I get closer to the team and listen. I make sure I don't jump to the conclusion that they are not talking about their reading. Let's say they are talking about going on their uncle's boat over the weekend. Should I assume this is not connected to their reading? Not necessarily. Maybe this child is reading about aquariums or beaches or someone's uncle. Therefore, I am careful about accusing children of wandering off the subject because part (really all) of reading is connecting to personal life and feelings.

Some questions of mine can help children remain connected to their reading:

Why are you reading that book?
What are you talking about? How is that connected to what you're reading?
Are you talking about your reading?

Remember, too, during team reading I circulate among all the teams as I listen and facilitate discussions.

QUESTION:

How do you keep a record of their reading? And how do you assess it?

ANSWER:

I keep a notebook where I jot down what each student is reading and writing. Children also keep records of their reading in a reading log where they sometimes write their reflections on the pieces they have just read. I periodically respond to these logs with questions and suggestions for future reading. Because homework is contextualized within the literacy issues discussed that day, it also amounts to a written record of the children's work. Of course their diary entries, too, form a record of each child's personal growth over time. I'll write more about this in a letter focusing directly on assessment.

QUESTION:

What about phonics?

ANSWER:

This is the question I am asked most. What about phonics? For some reason, many in our field believe that a battle rages between holistic instruction and phonics. A myth floating around suggests that teachers who believe in purposeful and meaningful reading avoid phonics. This question is also spawned I think by the entrenched belief that phonics is reading. But it is not. Phonics is a tool some may be able to use to help with decoding. Some children need this tool and use it successfully; others cannot use it at all. We need to apply phonics on an individual basis just as we, as good educators, do elsewhere. But do you think you might walk into my classroom and find me involved in a phonics lesson? How do I teach skills? In context or in isolation?
    If you answered yes, you're right. Believe it or not, you will see children involved in phonics in all areas of my program. As they write their drafts they are involved in purposeful phonics—deciding what symbols to write down for their ideas. In their diaries, logs and drafts of their presentations they are involved in phonics, actively and purposefully. So is there phonics in our community? Yes. But are the phonics lessons isolated, worksheet-oriented and discussed for a neat twenty minutes a day? No. Go back and skim the last letter where we talked

about the writers' workshop. Notice how much phonics takes place as children write and edit their drafts.

Phonics is present in many literacy discussions as I help edit children's work. Listen:

Nina:	Maria, you're ready to edit?
Maria:	Yes, Aurora already helped me first.
Nina:	Good. I see you're following the rule that we go to a friend first. Let's see. I like how you didn't worry about spelling while you were working on this draft and just wrote the word the best you could. Now, since you're finished with all your ideas, we can talk about how you've spelled some of your words. I like how you wrote "Mommy." Why did you write it this way: "Mme?"
Maria:	'Cause I heard the "em" sound and the "ee" sound.
Nina:	Yes, "em" just like the beginning of your name. Can I use your word to talk with the class about words that begin with em?
Maria:	Okay.
Nina:	Let's come together as a class for a minute. Thank you. I want to show you the great way that Maria spelled one of her words—Mommy. (I write Mme on the board.) Let's give her a hand for not worrying about spelling in the draft and just sounding it out the best she can. (Students clap.) Now let's talk about how we need to spell her word so that she can publish her story.
	What's the first letter of Mommy?
Steve:	"Em."
Nina:	Good. Let's think of other words that begin with "em." Raise your hand when you have some words and I'll write them on the board.
	(Students give words that begin with "M" and I write them on the board.) Now let's look at the last sound of Maria's word "ee." Momee.
	What letter did Maria use for the ending sound of Mommy.
Tasha:	"E."
Nina:	That's right. Does anyone know another letter that sometimes makes the "ee" sound? (No response.) Let's think of words that have the same ending sound like Mommy. Let's think. Oh, I just thought of one! We have a boy in this class who's name ends like Mommy. Think! Oh, I just realized, two boys!
Alba:	Danny!
Nina:	Yes, Danny-Mommy. Who else?
Billy:	Me!
Nina:	Yes! Billy-Danny-Mommy. (I write these words on the board as I say each one.) All these words have the same "ee"

Robin:	ending sound. But what letter do Billy and Danny end with? "Y."
Nina:	Right. So sometimes the "ee" sound at the end of a word is written with the letter "y." Mommy has the letter "y" at the end. Let's think of more words that end like Mommy, Billy, Danny. (Students come up with more words and then the class goes back to writing.)

I can just hear some of you protesting this is writing not reading! But writing is reading and reading is writing. Can you see why their division is false? If I want to connect the phonics skill to silent and team reading, I do it in the same way I connect any other skill:

Nina:	During silent reading I want you to look for some words that end with the same sound as Mommy, Billy and Danny. We can add these words to our list on the board. What other words can we look for?
Pooja:	Words that begin with the em sound.
Nina:	Okay. So we can add those to our other list. Let's begin reading. (Then after silent reading I resume) Now when you're in team reading I want you to share the words you've found and when we come together as a class we'll put them on our list.

Do I teach phonics skills? Yes! The same way I teach any other skill: in context and when needed. Please spread the word that teachers who teach within context do teach phonics. We need to make this clear to banish harmful myths. I need your help!

Let me end this chapter by encouraging you to think about reading and our reading instruction as a means of personal and political emancipation. When your classroom allows all learners full participation and responsibility, the boundaries come down and equal access to creative and transformative literacy becomes possible. In this way, we begin "the creation of a new attitude—that of dialogue, so absent in our own upbringing and education. . . dialogue in order to carry out education rather than domestication" (Freire, 1973, p. 52).

You've got lots to think about, I know,

Nina

Nina

P.S. I'm including a checklist that might help you organize some of the concepts in this letter. It is similar to the writing checklist I sent you, just focused more on reading.

Reading Process Checklist

_____ The children choose their own reading material.

_____ The children have a personal reading book with them at all times.

_____ The children read silently for a sustained and consistent time each day.

_____ The children discuss their personal reading in self-chosen teams (sometimes guided by team reading questions).

_____ The children have a separate reading log for systematic responses to readings and concepts taught in skills lessons.

_____ The children use T-Tell what you like, A-Ask questions and G-Give ideas (TAG) during their full-class sharing of personal reading.

_____ The teacher provides a wide variety of books for the classroom at all reading and interest levels.

_____ The teacher and all other adults in the classroom silently read with the children during sustained silent reading to model the importance of reading.

_____ The teacher or one of the children reads aloud daily an appropriate class-chosen book.

_____ The teacher keeps a log to note individual reading selections and progress.

_____ The teacher conducts five-minute skills lessons to the full class within the context of a child's personal reading and the class-chosen book.

LETTER #7
ALLOWING STUDENTS TO THINK: RETHINKING
"TEACHING STUDENTS WHAT TO THINK"

Radicalization involves an increased commitment to the position one has chosen.
It is predominantly critical, loving, humble, and communicative, and therefore a
positive stance. . . . He is convinced he is right, but respects another man's
prerogative to judge himself correct. He tries to convince and convert, not to crush
his opponent. The radical does, however, have the duty imposed by love itself, to
react against the violence of those who try to silence him.

(Freire, 1973, p. 10)

Dear Students,

Throughout our discussions of literacy and education, I ask you an enormous number of questions. You have also read the actual transcripts from my elementary school classroom and noticed most of my conversation consists of questions. Why do you think I do this? Well, what do my questions encourage you to do? I hope they encourage you to think. As you began this book you might have tried to skip over some of my many questions. Questions are easy to skim as you search for their answers. You found, though, that I leave some questions unanswered. Who says I have all the answers, anyway? Who says there's only one answer to a question? Who says there always is an answer? Have you ever come across questions without answers that are still worth asking?

If you've been exposed to more traditional instruction you are probably familiar with a system based on the belief that only one route leads to knowledge; each question has only one answer; and only one voice can provide that answer. I've said, teachers who see their students as empty vessels to be filled believe that they must give students the answers—must fill their students with the appropriate and correct knowledge.

I don't have all the answers. I do have my answers, though, and I believe in them passionately. But I wouldn't deny you your passion. You hear this passion in our discussions as I urge you to develop your own passion, your own voice. I try to do this with my questions. You, of course, must do most of the work. You must take the time to think of your answers to these questions. You might be ready to say, "I agree with everything she writes." That's fine with me, but you need to go beyond agreement to personal passion and belief. You must begin the inner dialogue with yourself and the open dialogue with your colleagues so that your mere agreement becomes conviction and part of who you are as a person and as an educator. Ultimately, the choice is yours and the major question you must come to grips with is not how you teach your students reading or writing but instead "Will I resolve to devote the time necessary for deep reflection on the crucial issues of schooling, philosophy and practice?"

The minute we begin thinking about these issues of differing questions and answers we end up having to redefine the teacher's role. When a teacher doesn't have all the answers, what happens? How does the conversation change in the classroom? Think about it. If they're not up there spouting out their knowledge, what could they be doing? Listening to others, to their students! And if they are lucky, they are both listening to them and learning from them.

One way we learn from people besides listening is asking them questions. But what kind of questions would we ask if we truly want to learn from someone we're interacting with? Would we ask the question we really are interested in or would we ask questions that we already know the answers to? Take a minute and think about this. Think about your past and present educational experiences. What kind of questions are you most accustomed to receiving in the classroom? Are they really important questions, or are they questions designed to measure your recall ability?

In the conventional classroom, the questions asked tend to be measurement devices for monitoring (1) how much students remember of the teacher's or the author's words, (2) whether or not you were listening, or (3) whether you did your homework. If you were one of the lucky ones in the highest reading group or an advanced program, you might have had the opportunity to answer more purposeful questions. Maybe. The view that we ask lower-level questions (focused on detail and comprehension) to lower-level students and higher-level questions to higher-level students is based on a hierarchical view of education. This view prevails throughout our educational system where we group students according to level and have them complete readiness activities before we move them on to the real thing. (We've already talked about this at great length in the last letter.) In fact, just as our children become leveled so do our questions.

I remember few of the details that I learned during my undergraduate teacher training program. For some reason, though, I remember a lot about this whole issue of questioning. Now that I think of it, maybe it was because I was bombarded with it (just as I was bombarded with Piaget's stage theory) in almost every undergraduate teaching course. Bloom's taxonomy—I can still see the chart and the order and labeling of the different types of questions. I remember when I did my field work, I had to write out the questions I planned to ask the children and make sure they followed Bloom's order. Now my stomach churns at the thought. Then I didn't know better and at that time I didn't reflect much either. Socrates once said the unexamined life is not worth living. I agree and complement his thought with my own: A teacher who refuses to reflect on his or her practice is no teacher at all—just someone who follows instructions. Unfortunately, as Giroux pointed out, "prospective teachers are taught methodologies that appear to deny the very need for critical thinking" (Giroux, 1988, p. 123).

Now I reflect deeply about everything I do and I find it really interesting to look back and analyze my early teaching. One video in particular I share with my undergraduate students shows me in my third year of teaching in the public schools. I am setting up the writers' workshop which, as you've read, is not based on levels or a predetermined hierarchy. But I hear myself responding to the children's work by asking the traditionally narrow questions that had become so ingrained during my undergraduate program and during my early years of teaching when I still relied on the teachers manuals:

Donniqua:	I like the way Rashia is ready. I like the way Eric is ready. My rabbit by Donniqua Duce: One day my rabbit went into the bush. My rabbit saw my mother. My mother said "Is this your rabbit?" I said, "Yes, mother." She said, "Where did you get it?" I said, "From school."
Nina:	Let's give Donniqua a hand for her story. (The children clap and then begin to raise their hands to respond.)
Donniqua:	(Picks one child) Lourdes.
Lourdes:	You could give your rabbit a name.
Nina:	Good idea, Lourdes.
Donniqua:	Ms. Zaragoza?
Nina:	What I really liked was Donniqua had talking in her story. Who was someone that was talking in her story? Eric?
Eric:	Her mother.
Nina:	Who else?
Jessica:	She was.
Nina:	That's right. What was one of the questions her mother asked?
Kendy:	Where did you get it?
Nina:	Right. Donniqua, why don't you read that question again? Let's find it. (I help Donniqua find it in her draft.)
Donniqua:	Where did you get it?
Nina:	Very good. That was one question. What was the question she asked before she asked "Where did you get it?" Her mother asked two questions. Let's put our hands down for just a second and let *every*body think. What was the question that her mother asked?
Donniqua:	(Choosing a child) Rashia.
Rashia:	Is this your rabbit?
Donniqua:	Very good.
Nina:	Exactly, and you said it in the exact words, Rashia. Let's look at this question again. Is this your rabbit? Was it Donniqua's rabbit?
Class:	Yes.
Nina:	Where did the mother see the rabbit?
Donniqua:	Monique.
Monique:	In the bush.
Donniqua:	Very good, Monique!
Nina:	What do you say to Donniqua, Monique?
Monique:	Thank you.
Tania:	What's your mother's name?
Donniqua:	Danielle.
Nina:	Danielle? I thought your mother's name was Tracy?
Donniqua:	She has two names!

Nina: Oh! Okay. So Danielle and Tracy is the same person, your
           mother. Thanks! Let's give Donniqua another hand. (The
           children clap as Donniqua sits down. Then Emilio comes up
           to share his draft. He is learning to speak English.)
Emilio: I like Rashia. I like Ezekiel. (All the children clap.)
Nina: Why do you like Ezekiel?
Emilio: He was sitting properly.
Nina: What? I can't hear you.
Emilio: He was sitting properly.
Nina: He was sitting what?
Emilio: Properly!
Nina: Properly! Wow! Where did you learn that word from?
Emilio: Mr. Leo (the English teacher).
Nina: Wow! I love how you used that word! I think Emilio deserves
           a hand! (Everyone claps.)

Look at some of the questions I asked in relation to Donniqua's story. Pretty
low level, don't you think? I mean really, how many more times could I have
repeated those questions her mother said? I definitely wasted time I could have
spent in more interesting conversation. I could try to justify some of it by saying
I was teaching sequence: "What was the question she asked before?" or teaching
Donniqua how to skim. But I don't think these reasons really do justify the use
of such inane questions. Almost every question was false. I knew all the answers
to the questions, so why bother asking? Of course we do this all the time with
children, this asking questions we already know the answers to. Children know
you know the answers and that you are just asking them to perform! How
condescending! How disrespectful! I think, I redeemed myself a bit when I
finally asked a question I didn't know the answer to. You can almost hear my
genuine surprise that Donniqua used the name Danielle for her mother instead of
Tracy.

I think with Emilio I am more genuine, too, I expressed admiration for his use
of the word "properly." I think, too, I showed Emilio that I was really interested
because I kept insisting he repeat himself until I finally heard what he was saying,
and I'm glad I did. What a great word! Notice, though, that I wavered between
real, genuine questions and lower-level detail and comprehension questions. At
that point I had yet to take the time necessary to make sure everything I do and say
consistently corresponds with my foundational philosophy. Perhaps I was still
developing this philosophy. As I read these early interactions over again, I do see
the beginnings of ideas now a central part of me and the classroom communities
I help create. Notice, for example, that Donniqua is in control as she praises the
children before she starts sharing and continues to choose children to respond to
her work. I also see the beginnings (the *very* beginnings) of contextualized
instruction as I pull from Donniqua's work. Do you see anything else? Well,
having the children clap for each other illustrates my incipient desire to strengthen
the community as we positively recognize each individual member. Finally, too,
running throughout this interaction is my early attempts to place children in
positions of power. They share their personal work in front of the entire

community, praise their classmates, and decide who will respond to their work. We all need to start somewhere.

I know you are by now accustomed to the way I interact with my students, but let me post just a small section of an interaction so we can examine it closer. I was reading aloud *Matilda* by Roald Dahl to the whole community, and I stopped throughout to question the students about the reading:

> Nina: Can you think of another word that means strange? (A few children raise their hands.) I'm looking for other people to participate. Jeff, we haven't heard from you yet.
> Jeff: Weird.
> Nina: Excellent! Any other words that are similar to weird or strange? Remember there is never just one right answer.
> Kit: Different.

I continued to read, then stopped to question the children again about Mrs. Trunchbill calling the children "stinkers":

> Nina: Would you like me to call you stinkers?
> Class: (They laugh and answer.) No!
> Nina: Why not?
> Ali: It's mean!
> Nina: Yes, and very disrespectful! (I continued to read and then stopped.) What do you think is going to happen to that car? (No response.) Think about Mr. Wormwood and the car. (No response.) What kind of cars does he sell? (No response.) Are they good?
> David: No, but he says they are.
> Nina: Yes, he cheats. So what do you think might happen to the car that Mrs. Trunchbill buys from him?
> Caroline: It might break down.
> Nina: Okay, I guess we'll see what happens! (I began to read again.)
> Nina: Do you think Matilda would do a trick like a stink bomb? (No response.) Think about Matilda and the tricks she's already done. Would she do a trick like a stink bomb?
> Alba: Yes, to get even.
> Nina: Okay. Ketty?
> Ketty: Yes, because she is upset.
> Guari: No, because she isn't *that* mean.
> Nina: Okay. Well we know that Matilda didn't do it but Mrs. Trunchbill doesn't. I think that because they've already said Matilda is brilliant she would do more complicated tricks. (I continued to read.)
> Nina: What's another word for "bellowed"? Hey, you can use this word in your writing if you want! Listen again: "You're darn right!" Mrs. Trunchbill bellowed. How does Mrs. Trunchbill talk? (No response.) Does she talk sweet and softly or loud?

Lourdes:	Loud.
Nina:	Okay. That's a hint. What does bellow mean?
Manuel:	Screamed.
Nina:	Good! Others? Remember there is usually always more than one answer! (Many children responded now with words like: "hollered," "yelled," "shouted." I continued to read.) What kind of character is Miss Honey? What type of personality does she have? (The children come up with words like "sweet," "nice," "caring," "kind," "gentle," "persistent.") Raise your hand if you are persistent. (Many raised their hands.)
	Yes, let's talk about some of the behaviors a person would show if they were persistent.
	(The conversation continued as I connected persistent behavior to children in the classroom.)

As you see there is a big difference between my questioning now and my questions relating to Donniqua's story. As we talked about *Matilda* I asked more genuine questions that encourage my children to think personally about the reading and the characters of the story. "Think about the kind of person Mr. Wormwood or Matilda or Miss Honey is." These types of questions make real connections with the characters and, in fact, the characters of *Matilda* became a part of our community. Indeed, genuine questions help form deep and genuine relationships between the author, the characters and ourselves.

Notice how I structure my questions. They usually begin very open-ended, then I narrow them as I pull for more response. Vygotsky called this "scaffolding" since each subsequent question supports the children more so they can answer successfully. I avoid limiting my questions in the beginning, though, because I want to avoid limiting my students' thinking. In fact, I offer little support in the beginning so that they have a chance to create a personal answer.

If you haven't guessed yet, I'm totally opposed to Bloom's famous taxonomy. As I tell my undergraduates, the way I instruct renders Bloom's taxonomy irrelevant. I encourage them to think deeply about the implications of using these questioning strategies that help neither children nor teachers to think. Under the guise of making sure that children understand them, teachers using this hierarchical form of questioning begin with such questions as

What color is the girl's dress?
What color is the boy's hair?
How old is the girl in this story?
How old is the boy in this story?
What happened to the girl?
Find the sentence that shows where the boy lives?
Where does the girl live?

After a dozen of these questions, how do you think the children will feel about the story? How would you feel? If you think you might feel bored, I guarantee you the children will. These questions are low level and, moreover, insulting. All of the answers appear in the text and require no real thought at all. Some well-intentioned teachers might answer me this way: "So? I do have to check whether they've read the story, don't I?"

I'll hold my complete answer for a little later. For now, let's assume you do need to check whether the children have read or listened to the story. The point is, can you do it in a more respectful and genuine way? Think about it. Try and reword the questions so that they still serve as a checking device but are more respectful and challenging. Let's try it:

- What color is the girl's dress? Why do you think the author decided to make the dress that color?
- What color is the boy's hair? Why do you think the boy's hair is blonde? Why is your hair brown?
- How old is the girl in this story? What would have happened if the girl were younger?
- How old is the boy in this story? What would have happened if the boy were older?
- What happened to the girl? Why do you think this happened?
- Find the sentence that shows where the boy lives. Would you like to live where he lives? Why or why not?
- Where does the girl live? If you wrote this story, where would you want the girl to live? Why?

Now, to the crux of the question: Do you really think we need to ask empty questions to check whether the children have read or listened to the material under discussion? Look at my rewordings. Don't they also monitor the task? They also invite children to think about the material as they make personal connections. I'm annoyed by the manipulation of teacher-student interactions and questions in order to control and monitor student thinking. If you want to find out if someone read a book you're interested in, what questions would you ask? You'd naturally ask such questions as "Did you read that book?" "How did you like it?" "Do you think I would like it?" Genuine and meaningful questions all, and anyone can answer them. I don't care who your students are, how society has labeled them, or how old they are. They can all answer genuine questions. "How do you like?" "What do you think?" "What was your favorite part?" "Why?"— everyone can answer. Unfortunately, according to Bloom and others—that is to say, those involved in the writing and marketing of mechanistic approaches to education—these types of questions should be asked only when students are "ready." I say that, in fact, all students deserve right from the beginning real and honest interactions that show respect for all. Let's have genuine questions that show children we truly are interested in them and in what they have to say.

Other Thoughts

While most of this letter focuses on the way in which we question our students, we have touched on an even deeper personal issue. Shouldn't we honestly question ourselves, our colleagues and the sacred stone-graven tenets that guide our profession? My previous letters reveal a strong tendency to question much of what I've heard during my years as a student and an educator. Who says we have to teach reading first? Who says that children have to be asked low-level questions before high-level questions? Who says that all children pass through the same stages?

I urge you to ask many of these "Who said?" questions. Don't be afraid to question Piaget, Dewey, Vygotsky, Bloom, your professors and yourself. When we question our children genuinely, we give them opportunities to think. When we question ourselves and our system we give ourselves opportunities to envision the future in a new way.

So what do you think?

Nina

Nina

LETTER #8
PLAYWRIGHTS IN ACTION: RETHINKING
POETRY AND DRAMA IN THE CLASSROOM

Dear Students,

As you can probably tell from my previous seven letters, our community spends lots of time creating and performing productions. When you think of it, it's an easy transition (it may not even be a transition at all) from authors of books to playwrights: just more stories! To get the children embarked on these productions, I immerse them immediately in the writers' workshop. As I strengthen their perceptions of themselves as authors, I give them several opportunities to express themselves verbally. As you already know, children share their work with the full community in many ways across the curriculum. They respond to each other's writing using TAG and I always encourage them to speak loudly, clearly and confidently.

In addition, I incorporate poetry in my classroom immediately so that the children become comfortable with verbal presentations. Now how do you think I introduce poetry? Remember, I try to make sure that all children feel successful, and I try to avoid potentially competitive situations. Thus, I avoid asking one individual child to read. As a matter of fact, I teach the poem before I even write it on chart paper (chart paper is the school supply which I use the most). How does this help ensure everyone's success? Well, if they already know the poem verbally, won't they be able to read it more easily when they see it in written form? Observe for a moment how I introduce the first poem in a second-grade classroom. Right after our morning song since the children are already standing, I decided to introduce this first poem:

Nina:	As long as you're standing let's learn a poem. It's a poem called "Dreams" by Langston Hughes. Has anyone ever heard of Langston Hughes? (No response.) He's a famous African American poet. He's one of my favorites. What is a poet?
Kelsey:	Like a writer.
Nina:	Exactly. A poet is a person who writes poems. Okay, listen. "Dreams" by Langston Hughes. Hold fast to dreams for if dreams die, life is a broken-winged bird that cannot __ . Oh who can guess what comes next? Listen again, hold fast to dreams for if dreams die, life is a broken-winged bird that cannot____ .
Children:	Fly!
Nina:	How did you know that?
Warren:	Cause it rhymes.
Nina:	Yes. What does fly rhyme with?
David:	"Die."

Nina: That's right. Let's say it together now. Ready, begin.

Most all: Hold fast to dreams for if dreams die, life is a broken-winged bird that cannot fly.

Nina: Excellent. Now listen to the next part. Hold fast to dreams for when dreams go, life is a barren field covered with____. What do you think the next word is. Shh. Let's give everyone a chance to think. Listen again. Hold fast to dreams for when dreams go, life is a barren field frozen with____.

Richard: Snow.

Nina: Yes, "go" and "snow." Now let's say that part together. Everyone.

All: Hold fast to dreams for when dreams go, life is a barren field frozen with snow.

Nina: Wow! You all know the poem already. Congratulations! Now let's look at the chart. (The chart was already up, but it was folded over so the words were out of sight. I unfold it so they are in full view.) Let's say it together as I point to the words. Ready, go!

All: "Dreams" by Langston Hughes. Hold fast to dreams for if dreams die, life is a broken-winged bird that cannot fly. Hold fast to dreams for when dreams go, life is a barren field frozen with snow.

Nina: Wow! Congratulations! You all stood so nicely. Why don't you sit for a minute. What kind of dreams do you think Langston Hughes is talking about?

Rene: When you go to bed.

Nina: Yes, that's one way we can think of dreams. What's another way? (No response.)
               What do you dream for yourself? What do you want to be when you grow up?

Tony: Policeman.

Nina: Oh, a police officer. Why do you think I said officer instead of man? (No response)
               Can a girl also be a police officer?

Keisha: Yes.

Nina: That's right, so we don't just say "man." (Here each child says what they want be when they grow up—nurse, singer, doctor, mother—as I briefly touch on concepts related to gender and choice.) So what Langston Hughes is talking about is what we dream for ourselves. Do you think it might be hard to become what you want to be? Angie, do you think it might take a while to go to school to be a doctor?

Angie: Yeah.

Nina: What do you think Langston Hughes is telling you? To give up and not try or to keep trying?

Angie: To keep trying.

Nina:	That's right. To hold fast and don't let anybody stop you from being who you want to be. Raise your hand if you are going to hold on to your dreams and not give up? (All the hands go up.) How do you think people feel if they give up?
Danny:	Sad.
Nina:	And how do you think a bird with a broken wing feels?
Ralitha:	Sad.
Nina:	Yes, that's why Langston Hughes put that sad bird in his poem. Does anyone know what barren field means? What do you think? (No response.) What kind of field would be sad, do you think? A field with flowers or one with no flowers?
Alonzo:	No flowers
Nina:	Yeah I think so, too, and that's what barren means—empty, sad. Remind me to write barren on a card so we can hang it up. We'll start putting all the new words we talk about on the bulletin board. Let's stand now and do the poem again. This time I want you to start thinking about what we can do with our bodies as we say this poem. You know our class does a lot of things on stage. Does anyone want to be an actress or actor when they grow up? (A few children raise their hands.) Well, you'll get a lot of practice in this class because we do some plays and we also practice our poetry so we can say it for the whole school. Maybe we can ask Ms. Barnes (the principal) if we can do "Dreams" over the loudspeaker on Friday!
Most:	(Excitedly) Yeah!
Nina:	I'm glad you're all so excited. Let's start thinking of movements for this poem. What can we do with our hands when we say "Hold fast"? Everyone do something so I can see your ideas. "Hold fast."

The children created movements as I said "Hold fast" and we decided which ones to incorporate. They could be one child's movements or a combination of two or more children's movement. Here most children clenched their fists for "Hold" and then clasped their crossed arms to their chest. In this way, we created movements for the entire poem.

Do you think this short session was enough for the children to learn the poem? Yes, most of them did and painlessly. Notice the number of times the children got to hear and recite the poem. Even before I showed the chart, most already knew most of it. In this way everyone felt successful and comfortable with the print. In fact, the print got introduced in an exciting and active way. All children were successful and supported as they read aloud together. If a child missed a word it was no big deal because another child was near to help. Did you notice, too, the contextualized instruction of vocabulary and concepts in relation to the poem? What a great way to learn! What do you think? I can tell you the students loved it.

Because we learn many poems by African American poets, I usually plan a poetry recital for February, African American History Month. But the children really honor African Americans throughout the year, not just in February. They learn a poem every one or two weeks, so you can imagine how many they can recite by February! Why do you think we begin to work toward a recital so soon? What message do we send the children about poetry when we learn it within the context of a recital preparation? What do we do for poetry itself when we connect it to a recital? You're right! The children memorize for a purpose: performance before a live audience. Recital time is exciting and rewarding. Everyone gets dressed up, families proudly aim cameras and camcorders, and brush their children's hair.

Frankly I've never met a child who did not enjoy poetry introduced in this way. As a classroom consultant, I've taught poetry this way to children I've never met before and they beg for more. Really. I've walked down the halls and children come up to me to recite a poem I've taught them or to ask, "Oh, come into our room today!" They absolutely love poetry. Once I asked a sixth-grade class why they liked poetry so much, and they decided it was because poetry was like music. Of course. It makes perfect sense.

By the end of September or the beginning of October, the children feel confident about speaking and reciting and so around this time we begin to write our first play. During my early years of teaching, I integrated drama into my literacy curriculum in the following way:

1.   The children suggest two or three fairy tales.
2.   The class votes on the fairy tale they want to dramatize.
3.   We read as a class various versions of the same fairy tale.
4.   As a class we adapt the play by putting it in our own words, adding characters and humor and a different setting. For example, last year the children adapted "Aladdin" and placed the story (very much changed!) within a 1950's setting.
5.   We create enough characters so that every child gets a speaking part.
6.   I guide discussion with a legal pad and pen in my hand to write down an initial script.
7.   I type up the script and give out copies to students to begin reading and editing.

The most difficult and time-consuming part of the process for me was facilitating the dialogue we needed for the adaptations to the tale we had chosen. After about five years, I realized why this was so hard. I had been contradicting one important principle of my philosophy, topic choice. I realized I had been imposing "a topic" on the children when I asked them to choose an already existing piece of literature. In fact, this restriction made it more difficult for the children to revise and adapt. Since they already carried media images of, for example, "Sleeping Beauty" or "Snow White," it was hard for them to break out and be creative. And I was worn out by the time we had a script written.

To conform to my writing process program, therefore, instead of beginning with an extant piece of literature, we started with absolutely nothing. Of course, when I reflect on what I just said, I realize a teacher never starts off with "nothing." All students and teachers come to a situation with an great deal of experience and feelings and opinions. And guess what? Finding a topic turned out to be incredibly easy. As a matter of fact, we decided on the main framework of the play in between 20 and 30 minutes.

Why do you think? Do you see how presenting an existing format or topic could be an actual hindrance to the writing? When this realization finally came to me, our productions became much more enjoyable and much less stressful for me. The following section lists the guidelines we use now.

Drama Productions

1. I solicit suggestions from the children.
2. We vote on an idea for a play.
3. We start writing script as a full class asking these questions:
   Okay, who will our characters be?
   What will the problem(s) be?
   What will the solutions be?
   Think about props.
   Think about music.
   (This process might take a month. The related homework might include: Write the setting for scene 1, and write the dialogue for scene 1.)
4. I type the script and make copies for each team.
5. The children read over the script to revise and edit it.
6. I copy the revised script for the entire class.
7. Enough copies are made so that each child can have a desk copy and a home copy.
8. The class reads the script aloud every day for about two weeks, and then we decide who plays the parts.
9. There are enough characters in the play so that each child says at least one line.
10. We use these criteria to assign parts:
    - If a child had a big part previously, he or she will not be chosen for a large part this time.
    - Children who need to participate more usually get their choice of parts.
    - Children who take care of their scripts usually get a first choice of part.
    - Children who memorize the script thoroughly tend to get their choices.
11. After the entire script is memorized, on-stage practice begins.
12. Students cue children, open and close the curtain and generally direct all aspects of practice.
13. Students help with scenery and dance steps.
14. Other teachers' help is solicited, i.e., music teacher, dance teacher, art teacher.
15. Programs are designed.

16. Play is performed in front of entire school and videotaped.

As you can probably guess, our class writes the play together within the context of a number of full-class discussions where I usually question them as I help facilitate the writing. After the general framework of the play is agreed upon, team discussions often center on adding details and dialogue.

Sample Dialogue During the Initial Script Development in the First Month of School

Who knows what a play is?

Who has seen a play? (Listen for responses and ask for examples.)

What do we act out? (The story.)

What do we call people who write plays? (Playwrights, or authors for plays.)

What do you think we are going to write? (A play !)

What is the first thing we need to think about? (An idea for our play.)

Focus on the idea that a play is also a story and contains such elements of a story as a main idea, a beginning, a middle, an end, problem(s) and solution(s), setting, and characters.

Connect these parts to real plays children have seen and make connections to the students' own writing.

In your teams, you need to think of the main idea of our play. Each team needs to agree on one idea. So when the class comes together how many ideas will we have? You might need to convince or persuade your teammates to use your idea.

Encourage the children to come up with ideas unconnected to their media experiences and to find original character names, situations, setting and so forth.

Write the team ideas on board, combining similar ideas.

Conduct a class vote on the remaining ideas, usually trying to combine ideas so that the class has three main ideas to vote on.

Initial Plan for Beginning a Third Grade Play

Title: *The Mystery of the Ghosts in the Third Grade*
(came from ideas formulated by the teams)

Problem and Solution

Beginning:
1. Things begin to disappear.
2. Things move by themselves.
3. Strange voices are heard.
4. Teacher blames students.

Middle:
1. Child says, "Maybe ghosts are afraid and that is why they don't come out"
2. Children leave notebooks, pens, pencils and candy out for the ghosts.
3. Children leave a tape recorder for the ghosts.

End:
1. Children write letters to ghosts saying, "We love you. Come visit us. Love, from, Ms. Alexis' class."
2. Ghosts walk into the class and the class asks, "Who are you?"
3. Ghosts say, "We're the ghosts. You helped us turn into third graders because you showed us that you cared."
4. Ghosts turn into third graders and become part of the class.

Setting:
A third grade in New York City.

Characters:
1. Teachers, Ghosts and Children.

THE MYSTERY OF THE GHOSTS IN THE THIRD GRADE

SCENE 1: Things Are Moving and Teachers Blame the Students

Ms. Vanessa:	What's happening?
Ms. Princess:	Why is everything moving?
Ms. Alexis:	You children are trying to trick us! Well not this time!
Debbie:	It's not us! We must be in the wrong classroom.
Dub:	Look how that book is moving!
Elizabeth:	Uh, oh, is this the right school?

Ms. Alexis:	Where is our grade book?
Ms. Princess:	We left it right here.
Ms. Vanessa:	Who took it!
Zack:	We didn't do it!
Ricky:	Uh, oh. What's happening?
Tommy:	This is really weird.
Ms. Vanessa:	You children are going to be in big trouble with your parents!
Ms. Alexis:	We mean it this time for real!
Jason:	Hey, we need to find out what is happening.

SCENE 2: Strange Voices

Peter:	Shhhh! I think I hear something. (Ghost song plays.)
Jennifer:	What is going on?
Scary:	OOH, OOH, OOH!
Wiggly:	Boooooo. Boooooo!
Ms. Princess:	You children are going to pay for this torture you are putting us through!
Kimberly:	I am scared. I think there are ghosts around us!
Trini:	Is this place haunted?
Rosemary:	Listen, I know there is something funny going on that we are not responsible for.
Jose:	We are being super quiet, but the ghosts are making noise again.
Baroca:	(in a loud voice) Oh, No!
Guile:	I think I am going crazy!
All Ghosts:	OOH, OOH, OOOOOOOOOOOH!
Sonic:	Where are all those creepy, bizarre voices coming from?
All Students:	Not from us!

SCENE 3: Things Disappear

Michelle:	Oh, my book disappeared!
Junior:	Mine too!
Eric:	So did mine!
Billy:	Am I dreaming? Let me check. (He pinches himself.)
Johnny:	Who is doing all this?
Laura:	I don't know. Let's ask the teachers.
Chris:	Why ask them, they keep blaming us anyway?
Jack:	It doesn't matter. We need to talk to her.
James:	O.K., let's do it!
Valerie:	Ms. Alexis, Ms. Vanessa, I think there are ghosts who are taking our things.
Veronica:	The ghosts must have taken your grade book also.
Ms. Alexis:	Stop telling me these strange stories

Thumbelina:	We are telling the truth. You have to believe us!
Debbie:	We are not trying to trick you!
Ms. Vanessa:	Go away! Stop making excuses for yourselves.
Dub:	I think we are going to lose our minds.

SCENE 4: Teachers Believe the Students

	(Teachers are in the class before the students arrive.)
Ms. Princess:	Today I am going to punish these students if anything goes wrong.
Ms. Alexis:	What a story these kids are trying to pull on us!
Ms. Vanessa:	We need to finish grading these papers.
Ms. Princess:	Let's go get some coffee downstairs first. (All three leave.)
Ms. Alexis:	Let me go back to grading those papers.
Ms. Princess:	Where are my papers?
Ms. Vanessa:	They were right here when I left the classroom.
Ms. Princess:	There are no students here yet.
Ms. Alexis:	Maybe they were telling the truth.
All teachers:	I can't believe I was blaming them for something they didn't do!

SCENE 5: Students Write to Ghosts and Ghosts Appear

	(Students come in.)
Ms. Princess:	Students, we need to apologize to you for not believing you.
Ms. Alexis:	This morning my papers disappeared and the classroom was empty.
Elizabeth:	Maybe the ghosts who are doing this are afraid to show themselves to us.
Ricky:	We should show them that we want to be their friends.
Tommy:	We can write them a letter inviting them to join our class.
Ms. Alexis:	That sounds like a good idea.
Jason:	Let's do it!

(The children write the letter and when they are finished read it aloud.)

October 31, 1994

Dear Ghosts,
Who are you? We would like to get to meet you. We don't wish you any harm. We are very friendly and wish that you would join our class. You can eat lunch with us, do projects with us, and become part of our class. We love you!

Love,
Our Third Grade Class

(Students leave letter for ghost along with some paper, pencils, candy and a tape recorder)

Peter: Let's leave this letter on the desk for the ghosts and paper and pencil so they can write to us.

Jennifer: Let's leave them some candy, too.

Kimberly: I hope they will meet with us tomorrow.

Trini: Put a note on the tape recorder so they will listen to our tape.

(Students leave everything out and go home. The Ghosts come and read the letter, eat the candy and listen to tape.)

Tape: Dear Ghosts, we want you to meet us at school tomorrow. We love you and want to be your friends. Give us a chance to prove to you that we care.

(The ghosts write a letter.)
(The next day the students read letter out loud)

Dear Students,
We are the ghosts. We were scared to come out because we thought that you would not accept us. We did not know that you loved us. We care about all the third graders in this class. We will meet you!
Love,
The Ghosts

Rosemary: I knew the ghosts were friendly.

Jose: Let's turn off the lights so they know to come in.

(They turn off the lights, and the ghosts come in and bring back the things they had taken.)

Halwen: We are so glad that you invited us into your classroom.

Spooky: We saw you having so much fun and wanted to be part of it.

Johnny: Come join our class and sit with us.

(Students and ghosts begin talking with each other.)

Elizabeth: Lets sing the "Hello Song" so we learn each other's names.

Initial Plan for Beginning a Third Grade Play

Title: *Melissa and Brian: Third Grade Inventors*
(came from ideas formulated in the teams)

Problem and Solution
Beginning:
1. The teacher puts the students into science groups.
2. Melissa and Brian become partners and begin making crazy inventions.

Middle:
1. They make a juice supposed to make them happy, but it makes them sad.
2. They make a cream supposed to make your hair grow, but it turns hair blue.
3. They make a pen supposed to make your handwriting neater, but it wets your paper.
4. They make sneakers supposed to help students run faster but instead they get glued to the floor. (The sneakers given to fastest runner in the school for a race get glued.)

End:
1. They make an ice cream machine that makes any flavor you want and has a computer.
2. The ice cream makes all the children smarter.
3. Everyone in the school is excited and claps for them.

Setting:
Tucson, Arizona

Characters:
Melissa and Brian, the third grade students and the teachers

MELISSA AND BRIAN: THIRD GRADE INVENTORS

SCENE 1: The Teachers Put Students into Science Groups

Ms. Janelle:	Good morning class. We will begin our science unit on inventing today.
Mike:	Wow, that sounds exciting!
Steven:	What will we be working on?
Ms. Stephie:	You will begin making your own inventions.
Mr. Ken:	The person sitting in front of you will be your partner.

(Students enthusiastically get together with their partners)

Brian:	Melissa, we get to be partners.
Melissa:	We will make great inventions.
Ms. Janelle:	Talk with your partners about the inventions you will want to make.
Ms. Stephie:	The whole class can share ideas.

SCENE 2: Students Begin Discussing Inventions

Givoli:	Let's make a creature or something we both like.
Sasha:	We need to think about this.
Dennis:	Can we make some toys?
Charles:	Let's make something for other kids.
Michael:	How about a machine that makes chocolate?
Rocky:	That sounds yummy!
Tom:	We have so many choices that this is going to be a tough choice.
Kelly:	I wonder what Brian and Melissa are going to make?
Katherine:	Let's ask them.
Tommy:	Hey Brian, what are you and Melissa making?
Brian:	It's a surprise. But it is for everyone to use.
Angela:	Wow, that sounds mysterious!

SCENE 3: Juice Supposed to Make You Happy but Makes You Sad

Melissa:	This juice is great!
Brian:	This juice will make everyone smile.
Jacob:	What is that?
Melissa:	This is a juice we invented that makes you smile.
Jennifer:	Can we try some?
Brian:	Sure! Here you go.
David:	It tastes a little funny.
Daniel:	I know it does.
Charlie:	(Cries)
Tatiana:	Why are you crying?
Charlie:	I don't know.
Dennis:	Drink the juice Melissa and Brian invented. It will make you smile.
Charlie:	I did! That's what made me cry, I think!
Mr. Ice:	Oh, no! Why does everyone look so sad?
Jessica:	We drank Melissa and Brian's juice and it made us sad.
Mr. Jerry:	I thought that juice was called Happy Juice and was going to make people smile.
Laura:	We need to change its name then.
Lisa:	Call it Depressing Juice.

Melissa:	Brian, something has gone wrong in our juice.
Brian:	No joke, Melissa.
Melissa and Brian:	Back to the science table!

SCENE 4: Cream Supposed to Make Hair Grow but It Turns Hair Blue

Jan:	I know why your juice didn't work. Maybe you weren't meant to make juice.
Mike:	You were meant to make hair cream.
Melissa:	Hair cream?
Steven:	Yeah, cream to make your hair grow.
Brian:	Oh yeah, this cream can be for people who don't want short hair.
Mr. Ken:	Wow class, I am sure Melissa and Brian appreciate your help.
Brian and Melissa:	(Work on their cream.) Here is our finished product.
Melissa:	Who wants to be the first one to try it?
Stephanie:	I will!!
Brian:	Great!
Melissa:	Soon you will be able to braid your hair. (Starts putting cream on Stephanie's hair and the curtain closes.) (Curtain opens and Stephanie has a towel on her head. Brian and Melissa, ready to take off the towel, have a mirror in their hands the students look shocked as towel is removed.)
All:	OOOOOH!
Stephanie:	(With blue hair) Why is everyone looking at me?
Givoli:	Don't panic!
Stephanie:	What happened? Give me that mirror!
Melissa:	You l-l-l-o-o-k. . .
Brian:	It's, It's, It's. . .
Stephanie:	Oh no, give me that mirror. Now! (She screams.) AAAAHHHH!
Sasha:	I think there might be a problem!!!
Dennis:	This calls for some major hair dying!
Brian and Melissa:	Back to the science table!

SCENE 5: Pen That's Supposed to Make Handwriting Neater but Instead Wets the Paper

Brian:	Let's make a pen.
Melissa:	What's so great about a pen?
Brian:	Nothing if it's a regular pen. But we will invent a very special pen. A pen that makes even the sloppiest handwriting neat.
Melissa:	Okay. Let's do it!

Brian and Melissa:	(after working) Here, class, is a pen that makes your handwriting neater.
Charles:	Mmmm. Should we try it?
Michael:	What harm could a pen do?
Rocky:	Okay. I'll try it.
Tom:	Me, too.
Kelly:	I need it, too. My handwriting needs to improve.
Katherine:	Watch how I write this sentence.
Tommy:	Oh no! His paper is wet! Not again!
Melissa and Brian:	We know, we know. Back to the science table!

SCENE 6:   Shoes That Are Supposed to Make Students Run Faster but Instead Make Them Run Slowly

Melissa:	We have a foolproof plan.
Zack:	Are you sure it will work this time?
Brian:	Positive!
	(They work at the science table.)
Angela:	Those look like sneakers.
Melissa:	Yeah, but they aren't just ordinary sneakers.
Brian:	They make you run faster
Jacob:	What harm can sneakers do?
Jennifer:	I don't know. . . .
David:	Let's give the sneakers to Tammy, the fastest runner in the school.
Daniel:	Yeah, even if they don't work, she still runs fast.
Charlie:	She can wear them in the race.

SCENE 7:   Tammy Races in the Slow Sneakers

	(Close curtain and open it. Tammy in race with the sneakers. Hear: "On your mark, get set, go.")
	Tammy runs very slowly and loses.
Students:	Oh well. Maybe Melissa and Brian should try something else!

SCENE 8:   Make Computerized Ice Cream in Any Flavor and It Makes You Smarter

Melissa:	Since we've done so many harmful inventions we should apologize by making ice cream for the whole school.
Brian:	This machine will do it all.
Melissa:	Let's put it in the cafeteria but not tell anyone it was us.
	(Puts in cafeteria and the students begin using it.)
Tatiana:	This machine is cool it makes ice cream. Any flavor! I love it!

All students:	Me too!
Dennis:	You know since I've been eating the ice cream in the cafeteria I feel smarter.
Jessica:	I do, too.
Jerry:	Whoever invented this did a great job!
Laura:	I saw Melissa and Brian put it in the cafeteria the other day.
Lisa:	We have to tell them the good news about the ice cream.
Janelle:	We have to tell everyone in the school.
	(Students begin telling each other. Close curtain.)

SCENE 9: All in Front of School Clapping

Melissa and Brian:	Why is everyone clapping?
Mike:	You made the best invention in the world.
Students:	(scream) Thank you!
Melissa and Brian:	Sorry for all those crazy inventions we made.
All Students:	That's okay. We know you tried your best. And this ice cream is great.
Steven:	Yeah, we're all getting A's on our tests and doing the best we can in everything!
Melissa and Brian:	At least we don't have to go back to the science table!

In each stage of development each play changed, and these changes happened within the context of writing and practicing the play. Within this context, too, we continued to discuss such writing conventions as punctuation, beginning, middle, end, setting, and whatever else we needed to discuss as playwrights. Here, again, we see a useful way to contextualize and personalize skills instruction. In fact, when the initial script circulates, I usually overlook grammatical conventions so that children get opportunities to edit in the context of drama. Of course, the social issues raised in relation to the plays never end. Read through the plays above and think about what types of conversations these plays could facilitate. What did you come up with? I think the play about ghosts easily promotes discussions about school and teacher expectations and trust. It also promotes serious discussion about the relationships between teachers and students and newcomers in the community. The play about the inventors Melissa and Brian lends itself to issues of gender and accomplishments.

As we rehearse our plays, we construct new ideas and make additions. Children are free to alter their lines—to make them longer or shorter according to their personal desires. How does this flexibility fit with my philosophy? What message do we send students when we allow such involvement?

Yes, a larger number of choices and a lot of personal involvement comes into play here as well. As usual, I discourage dependence on the teacher and promote instead independence and community dependence. Thus, I quickly turn over all aspects of the production to the students. Students become the directors, randomly for the beginning productions and then, when we know each other well, we make a community choice. For example, we chose Henry as our director for one of our end-of-year productions because we all agreed that Henry needed to practice talking louder and more assertively. I guide the directors in the following way:

Nina:	So what is the job of the director?
Alex:	To tell people what to do.
Nina:	Okay. Let's say more about that.
Jan:	If like someone forgets their words, the director tells them.
Nina:	Okay. What else does a director do?
Maggie:	Like tell the kids where to stand.
Nina:	Good. So the director helps with staging, too. Does the director only pick out the things that are wrong? (No response.) How can the director help the actresses and actors feel good about themselves? Think about what we do in writing.
Mitch:	Tell what you like.
Nina:	That's right. We tell what we like so our friends feel good about what they've written. What's that word we use when we say something nice about what a person does? (No response) I'm thinking of a word that starts with "pr—."
Mari:	Praise!
Nina:	Yes, that's the word I was thinking of. Can anyone think of another word?
Jeff:	Recognize.
Nina:	Good! I like that word. So the directors also have to recognize the performers when they are trying their best. What are some of the things that the director will have to remind a performer to do. Think about how we need to say our poetry.
Christy:	Talking loud
Nina:	The director needs to say "Louder." What else?
Nora:	Slower.
Nina:	Good! Let's write these down so we remember.

The conversation continues until we create guidelines to help our directors. The directors write down these guidelines to help them do their job effectively. And they are *very* effective.

What directors need to tell performers:

louder
slower
more expression
move your body
look at the audience
very good!
excellent!

In general we write a fairly uncomplicated play to perform during the first part of the year and a more complicated play that includes more props, music and costumes for an end-of-year performance. By the time we begin planning for the last production, the children are independent enough to do practically all of the work. Children open and close the curtains, change the scenery (which they create) and cue performers. In fact, I make sure to stay away from behind the scenes during the production. I once tried to help during a scene, found myself more nervous than the children, and almost had them open the curtain at the wrong time! Now during a performance I am in the audience fully trusting the students to do their best. I am never disappointed.

Meanwhile, I keep in mind some major principles as I work with my class on developing and producing a play for later performance. First of all, everyone in my class gets to speak at least one line in the play. This participation is extremely important for my literacy program because drama is an integral part of our literacy environment. Therefore, all children must be involved in as many aspects of the production as possible. If I used participation in the play as a privilege, I would actually be denying literacy instruction. Do I have a right to do that? Do I have a right to deny math or science or social studies instruction to students? No more than I have a right to deny a student full participation in a stage production.

"Full participation" does not mean the "same participation," however. Just as in all teacher decisions I keep uppermost in my mind the need for all children to feel successful and safe. Therefore, full involvement for one child might be three lines, and to another child it might be three words. In fact, allowing the children to adjust their own parts gives them all a say in their success.

Now you may have been wondering "How in the world are the parts assigned anyway?" I bet you know me well enough by now to guess the traditional audition has no place in our classroom. Why do you think I avoid auditions? What message would I send the children if I held auditions? Do you think that my ultimate goal of a play production is a perfectly performed play, or do I have wider literacy goals for these productions?

Remember, that what I try to achieve with each decision I make is to raise cooperation over competition in all our classroom interactions. In fact, I work to eliminate all competition in my classroom. As I've mentioned before, I see myself as a social change agent, and I provide a classroom that mirrors how I believe society should be. As Gandhi once said, "Be the change you want to see." I believe that competition which is so much a part of our society and our school systems is unhealthy for our children, and I continually try to eliminate it from my classroom. Competition makes one child's success dependent on another child's failure. These types of inherent comparisons are disrespectful and painful. All children can be successful in their own ways, so it makes sense to eliminate comparisons between children from the classroom. Auditions would, therefore, contradict much of what I believe. So what do I do?

Actually, parts can be assigned in a number of ways. How would you keep competition and negative comparisons out of the picture? Early in the year when we work on our first play, we usually choose the parts randomly. Either we draw names from a hat or use the class list to assign parts. For example, if Vanessa's name were first on the list, she would play the first part on the script. Jose would be given the second character if he were second on the list. If Jose's part were written for a girl, we would rewrite the part so that a boy is comfortable playing it. If we have too few parts to cover the whole class (even though we start writing the play with the question, "How many characters do we need so that everyone gets to say something?") we write in the extra parts we need.

Once the parts are assigned, all the children have a script for at least a week or two of study, and "Study script" becomes part of the nightly homework. While we generally work on the development of the script as a class, I sometimes assign refinements for homework. For example, one homework assignment connected to "The Mystery of the Ghosts in the Third Grade" was to write the friendly letter to the ghosts. In fact, this was purposeful homework because the letter incorporated into the final script came from one student's homework assignment. What other assignments can you think of that might purposefully connect to the development of the script?

Sample Homework Assignments Connected to Drama Productions

1. Write the children's letter to the ghost. Make sure you put in a greeting and a closing.
2. Pick a setting for the play and defend your choice.
3. Think of the name that you want your character to have in the play. Make sure it's a name you love!
4. Make a list of the props we will need for the play.
5. Write dialogue for the play.
6. Draw a picture of the stage design for each scene.

For our second or third productions we use background information to help us assign parts. If Tasha was Melissa in our first play, should she be the lead in our second play? Why or why not? Remember, consider your answer in the context of my classroom and my philosophy. Do I really care to have a perfect play? ("Oh Tasha did such a fine job as Melissa and she has all that experience. She will make an excellent lead again!") Or do I have wider literacy goals in mind?

By now you know that I use the play as one vehicle for exploring literacy; therefore, literacy development is my goal, not perfection. Tasha would not get the lead in the next play for a number of reasons. Here are two: First, it wouldn't be fair to the others who did not have the lead. Second, Tasha had the opportunity to develop her oral skills and now another needs this opportunity. What other reasons can you think of to give another child the lead in a subsequent production?

As children begin to feel safe and confident, their oral development improves dramatically. In fact, children who were "quiet" and introverted at the beginning of the year often become the characters with the most lines in our final productions. How do you think this happens? Well, throughout the year all children work on gaining confidence and assurance. All their activities are connected to sharing (TAG) and oral development (individual presentations), and they become comfortable expressing themselves. Some children need to be encouraged more than others to express themselves orally. Indeed, one of our ethical duties as teachers is to support our students so that they develop oral expression fully. Therefore, in our subsequent plays, I might encourage the more introverted students to try the lead: "Mary, would you like the part of _____? Why don't you go home and think about it and if you want that part tell us tomorrow."

At other times I offer a choice of parts to some "quiet" students and get surprising results. For example, Douglas, a boy who had difficulty sharing orally, had the choice of any part in our final production he wanted. To our great surprise, Douglas picked the male lead of the play, and it was a fantastic performance.

Imagine if I had decided against giving Douglas a choice. It would have been easier, after all, for me to assume that Douglas would be more comfortable with a smaller part since he speaks softly and infrequently. But this assumption would have limited him and his oral development. The choice gave him a chance to challenge himself and reach his fullest potential.

Randall, a second-grade student, just before the performance of our first production, *Sleeping Beauty*, cried so hard his mother had to take him home. In our last production of the year, *Peter Pan*, Randall had a speaking part, the father. He happened to be my student in third grade as well, and guess what part he took in our year-end production of *Wizard of Oz*? The Tin Man! And he even sang a musical solo.

While my children follow a schedule every day that contains more or less the same elements, it also remains flexible enough for other forms of literacy to become part of our literacy community. For a number of reasons I make sure always to offer a variety of reading projects. One important reason is boredom! I want to have as much excitement and fun in my classroom as my students do. Can you imagine doing the same thing day in and day out for 180 days? I can't. Actually, I decided to become a teacher partly for the opportunity to make my job as exciting as I want it to be. And that's exactly what I've done! To maintain excitement and enthusiasm we continually read and add new pieces to our literacy community. We save a lot of these pieces on video, and they are still being viewed—and not just by me and my undergraduates. I recently met one of my past third-grade students, now in eighth grade, and the first thing he told me was,

"Hi! I watched *The Wizard of Oz* with Jennifer last week! My lion costume was funny!"

Before I close let me mention another literacy activity that is now a major part of our community: letter writing. My students become very fluent letter writers as they correspond with other students in Michigan, South Carolina, Pennsylvania and our own community. Just as in any other form of writing, my letter-writers go through the same process: first forming their ideas, then seeking assistance with spelling, punctuation, grammar, and so forth. As usual, a real purpose accompanies every letter, whether it is a thank you note, an invitation to one of our plays or recitals, or a long distance conversation. As you can tell by the format this book takes, letter writing is one of my favorite forms of writing. The intimate informality of the friendly letter helps me and my students get our thoughts on paper.

I'll write soon,

Nina

Nina

P.S.   I've enclosed one more play we wrote, "Adventures in Discovering the Four Habitats." Notice that it is content based? It is a good example of how naturally we can integrate language arts, social studies and science. Drama presents an ideal way to integrate content areas. Read over this play and see how much research went into it. When you teach social studies and science, you can do it in an isolated way or in a purposeful and meaningful way. I bet you can guess what choice I hope you will make.

ADVENTURE IN DISCOVERING THE FOUR HABITATS
WRITTEN FEBRUARY 1995

SCENE 1:   **Marjory Stoneman Douglas Elementary School: Third Grade Class**

	(Open curtain. We see adventurers reading silently).
Adventurer 6:	Wow, we just read a lot about Marjory Stoneman Douglas. Did you know that she's helping to save the Everglades?
	(Close curtain.)

SCENE 2: The Everglades

	(Open curtain.)
Panther:	I'm going to bother the alligator.

Alligator:	Don't even think about it.
	(Panther and Alligator look hungrily at Eagle.)
Eagle:	Ha. Ha. Ha. You guys are funny. *(But the eagle is scared.)* Bye, I'm going to spy on something.
Deer:	I'll just sit here on the rock and watch you two being silly.
	(Flamingos are standing together.)
Flamingo 1:	I'm going to eat.
Flamingo 2:	Me too. Let's go. Bye everyone.
Eagle:	Wait! Look over there! I see something!
	(On the other side of the stage are the adventurers.)
Adventurer 3:	Wow! How did we get here? Look, we're in the Everglades.
Adventurer 5:	Cool! What are those pink looking birds with long legs?
Adventurer 2:	I think they are called flamingos.
	(A hanging doll of an eagle flies in circles)
Adventurer 6:	Look at that thing circling the sky. What is it?
Adventurer 1:	Could it be a plane or a football?
Adventurer 2:	No! It's an eagle. Look how big its wings are.
Adventurer 5:	I think I see an alligator and a panther. Those are meat eating animals. I think we'd better get out of here.
Adventurer 1:	Look! The alligator is approaching us! Run!
	(Adventurers start running.)
Alligator:	Wait, stop running! I won't eat you! Stop!
Miccosukee Indian:	Yes. Stop running. These are our friends. They won't hurt you.
	(Adventurers stop running, turn toward the alligator, but look scared.)
Alligator:	Where did you come from and where are you going?
Adventurer 6:	We were talking about Marjory Stoneman Douglas and how she saved the Everglades, and all of a sudden we appeared here.
Miccosukee Indian:	Who is Marjory Stoneman Douglas?
Adventurer 2:	She is a lady who fought very hard to save the Everglades so that it wouldn't be used for buildings but for homes for the animals that live there.
Flamingo 1:	Well, since you're here already, come and we'll show you our home.
Flamingo 2:	Yeah, our home that is getting smaller because of all the draining of the water to be able to build more homes for people.
Alligator:	There are so many people that keep taking our home and all we can do is move to some place with more water.
Panther:	Some people let the pesticides or insect killers go into the lakes and rivers where the fish can drink it. And

when my panther friends eat a fish, they get poisoned too!

Deer: Let's show you how beautiful the Everglades is and maybe you could help save the Everglades too like Marjory Stoneman Douglas has helped.

(Adventurers and animals walk along the Everglades.)

Adventurer 4: Wow! This place is wonderful!

Flamingo 1: Yeah!

Adventurer 5: I never knew it could be so beautiful looking through the eyes of animals.

Adventurer 6: I am going to think of ways to help save the Everglades and do it.

Adventurer 3: What type of animal is that? It looks like a different type of cat.

Panther: That's a relative of mine. But it doesn't live in the Everglades.

Adventurer 1: I know what it is! It's a jaguar! It belongs in the rain forest.

(Close curtain.)

SCENE 3: The Rain Forest

(Open curtain.)

(Adventurers look bewildered. Toucan, Macaw, Anteater, Python are on stage).

Adventurer 4: Look! Now we're in the rain forest!

Adventurer 5: Look at all the animals! That colorful bird with that large beak must be a Toucan.

(Danny the Yanomami Indian walks with his pets Zachary, the leopard and the jaguar, Chris. Danny has an arrow in his hand.)

Yanomami Indian: *(Talking to leopard and jaguar)* Let's go hunt for food.

Zachary (Leopard): *(Talking to Chris)* Isn't the rain forest nice? It does not have any danger. Mmmm, I'm hungry. Let's go snack.

Chris (Jaguar): *(Running)*Mmmm! I hope we're going to the river to hunt for fish. Let's go.

Janet the Toucan: Wwwaka. Wwwaka. Wwwaka. I see some strangers in the rain forest.

Melissa the Macaw: *(Standing in a tree)* Look at those adventurers. Look at them, just look at them!

Zachary (Leopard): Chris, get ready to pounce on them.

Vanessa the Python: No, they might be friendly!

Erik the Anteater: *(Walks on stage looking for ants to eat)* Has anybody seen any ants around? What is all this commotion? What's going on?

Vanessa the Python:	*(Slithering on the stage)* Yesssss, what'ssss going on? *(Danny the Yanomami Indian walks toward the adventures, introduces himself and invites them to his home. Chris and Zachary are growling.)*
Danny:	*(To his pets)* Calm down. Easy now. *(To the adventurer)* Welcome to the Amazon rain forest! Where do you come from?
Adventurer 4:	We come from Miami, Florida. What a wonderful and interesting place the rain forest is. Look at all the wild life.
Danny:	Yes, it is marvelous. Would you like to see our home here in the Amazon rain forest?
All Adventurers:	Yes. Definitely. Sure.
	(Danny and the Adventurers walk to other side of stage where the Yanomami Indians live. When they get there, the other Yanomami Indians are there. They greet the adventurers kindly).
Yanomami Indian 1:	Welcome to our home.
Yanomami Indian 2:	Come, sit with us. We will eat now.
Adventurer 5:	Oh, thank you.
Adventurer 3:	This is very different from our home.
Adventurer 4:	Everyone in the world has different homes depending on where they live.
	(Yanomami Indian serves the adventurers and other Yanomami Indians food.)
All Adventurers:	Wow, I have never tried anything like this. It's great!
Adventurer 6:	I am still hungry!!! I wish I had some dessert!
	(Close curtain.)

SCENE 4: The Desert

	(Open curtain. Adventurers appear.)
Adventurer 6:	Desert? I said dessert!
Adventurer 5:	We're in the middle of nowhere! Sand everywhere!
Adventurer 4:	Look there's a city way over there! I can almost see it!
Adventurer 3:	Don't get fooled, it might be a mirage.
	(Animals are in the city.)
Tommy the Camel:	I am getting bored. I want to go somewhere. Who will come with me to find something to do?
Kimberly the Iguana:	I will. I like to get away from the city sometimes.
Sub-zero Scorpion:	I want to do something really fun! I want to pinch someone.
Turtle:	I'll stay with Scorpion.
Roadrunner:	This is really boring. I'll go too.
	(Camel, Iguana, and Roadrunner go out of the city.)
Roadrunner:	Who are those people over there? They look lost.
Tommy (Camel):	Yes, I wonder why they are here.

Kimberly (Iguana):	Do you think they just appeared here?
	(Camel, Iguana, and Roadrunner walk up to the adventurers.)
Tommy (Camel):	What are you doing here?
Roadrunner:	Where did you come from?
Adventurer 1:	Out of nowhere.
Adventurer 4:	We come from Marjory Stoneman Douglas Elementary School. We need water.
Tommy (Camel):	Here, I could give you some of my stored water.
Adventurer 6:	Thank you, you're a very kind camel.
	(Turtle and Scorpion are coming)
Adventurer 5:	Look! It's a turtle and a scorpion. Let's get out of here, the scorpion will poison us.
Kimberly (Iguana):	Don't worry, they won't do anything.
Tommy (Camel):	Yeah, because I know them, they are my friends. *(Talking to the scorpion)* Hi.
Sub-zero Scorpion:	Hey, Mr. Camel. Hello, my friends. Who are these people?
Adventurer 4:	We are adventurers.
Roadrunner:	Why do you call yourselves adventurers?
Adventurer 2:	Because we are discovering the four habitats and having many adventures.
Tommy (Camel):	What kind of adventures?
Adventurer 1:	Well, we went to. . .
Adventurer 3:	Shhhh!!! Don't say the other habitats!
Adventurer 4:	Why not?
Adventurer 6:	You can't say those words because we'll go back there again and we want to stay in the desert.
Adventurer 5:	But, I am really boiling hot, though. I would love to have a good swim in the ocean! *(Close curtain.)*

SCENE 5: The Ocean

	(Open curtain. Adventurers are on a raft in the middle of the Atlantic Ocean.)
Adventurer 6:	Hey! We're in the ocean! How did we get here?
Adventurer 4:	Because someone said "ocean."
Adventurer 1:	And how did we get into this raft?
Adventurer 2:	I'd rather be on a raft than drowning.
Max the Whale:	I'm hungry for fish! I need to eat four tons of food a day. That's all I do: eat and swim, eat and swim.
Dolphin 1:	I want to swim and play.
Dolphin 2:	Yes, I want to play too.
	(Dolphin 2 looks up and sees a shadow.)
Dolphin 2:	What is that shadow up there?
Max:	It looks like a raft full of people. They look awfully fishy compared to us.

	(Shark comes swimming by.)
Dolphins 1 and 2:	AAHHH. Swim!
Shark:	Give me some dental floss so I can sharpen my teeth to get a bite out of that raft.
	(Shark bites the raft and adventurers fall into the water.)
Shark:	Dinnertime!
	(Shark swims after adventurers and runs into Dolphin 1.)
Dolphin 1:	AAHHH! Shark!
Orca Whale:	I'm going to pick up those people up because they look tired. I'll take them up for air since I need some too.
Adventurer 6:	Where are we going?
Orca Whale:	Where do you live?
Adventurer 4:	We live in Florida.
Orca Whale:	O.K. I'll take you to the Florida Keys.
	(Orca Whale takes adventurers to the Florida Keys and drops them off.)
Orca Whale:	Here we are.
All Adventurers:	Thank you so much! I don't know what we would have done without you.
Adventurer 5:	Look at that manatee. Wow. Did you know manatees swim in waters where rivers come out of? Yeah, like the "River of Grass," the Everglades!
	(Close curtain.)

SCENE 6: The Everglades

	(Open curtain.)
Adventurer 3:	Aren't these Everglades beautiful? We're lucky to live so close to them. I am glad people are now beginning to take care of them! Thank you Marjory Stoneman Douglas!
Adventurer 1:	There's no place like Marjory Stoneman Douglas Elementary School. There's no place like Marjory Stoneman Douglas Elementary School. There's no place like Marjory Stoneman Douglas Elementary School.
	(Close curtain.)

SCENE 7: Marjory Stoneman Douglas Elementary School: Third Grade Class

	(Open curtain.)
Adventurer 4:	This adventure was amazing.
Adventurer 2:	Yes, it was. And we were able to learn so much about

the different habitats.

Adventurer 5:   But I'm glad we're back. Now we can learn more about other things and maybe have more adventures.

LETTER #9
AUTHENTIC EVALUATION:
RETHINKING THE FRIDAY SPELLING TESTS

When children use a temporal framework to examine their achievements (and the feelings of self-worth that are attached to these achievements), they contrast their ability to accomplish something now with their previous inability to accomplish it. As children reach the age of three or more, they develop a sense of history, and they realize that what they could not do yesterday they can do today, and what they cannot do today they will be able to do tomorrow. When children's understanding of their achievements is supported by those close to them, these comparisons become satisfying and pleasurable. . . . However, this temporal notion of achievement begins to weaken just as children enter school age. . . whereas a preschool child in the United States might ask, "Can I do it better than I did before?" a child during the early school years begins to ask, "Can I do it better than the other children in my group?" Unless elementary schools consciously attempt to balance this "comparative" framework and offer more collaborative notions of self-achievement it will be difficult for most children to develop attitudes and values consistent with critical democracy.

(Goodman, 1992, p. 136)

Dear Students,

If there is one routine that seems more entrenched in our schools than most it is that Friday spelling test. How would our classrooms function without that spelling test? While it seems like a simple activity, it symbolizes many of our assumptions about assessment and children's failure and success. The question I urge you to consider is "Why do we give spelling tests?" Remember, if you see yourself as a decision maker, your reflection upon these questions of mine will be crucial to the development of your philosophy and the interaction that will one day take place in your classroom.

As both a university professor and an elementary school teacher, I think about assessment a lot more than I wish too! As I've thought about assessment issues over the years, I've come to realize that everything I talk about and everything I do relates to assessment. It's a paradox, I know, but a couple of years ago this fact came crashing down upon me as I team-taught an integrated language arts, reading and social studies course with two university colleagues. The course was experimental and exciting because for the first time our college students would have a chance to learn these courses within an integrated format—and in a format, incidentally, school systems have begun to use in elementary instruction.

I was glad to be involved in such a venture because I believe in this kind of integration. I also looked forward to teaching with two colleagues I had yet to work with. We met often to form the structure and content of the course and had an easy time of deciding the topics and content for each session. We divided up our assignments well, and each of us took responsibility for "our" individual assignments. For example, I took responsibility for a reflection paper on psychological and pedagogical philosophy (you might have guessed!) and on helping a child work through the writing process. I was also instrumental in incorporating reflection logs that required our students to reflect on class experiences and readings. Beverly's assignments were focused more on social studies, and Natalie's was focused more on reading comprehension and strategies.

Everything seemed to be progressing well until we returned our second assignment. I had responded to the first assignment, a reflection on philosophy. I respond to reflective work with written comments and questions. If the students seemed to have done an adequate job, I gave them full credit. If not, I asked them to resubmit their work addressing my feedback and this resubmission earned them full credit. Natalie evaluated the second assignment and she gave the students numerical scores like 8.5/11. When the students asked to resubmit improved papers for higher grades, she refused them the opportunity.

Beverly's assessment strategy fell between Natalie's and mine. While she gave numerical scores, she also included corresponding written explanations. At this point, I began to realize we were going to have some conflicts. And we did. As the semester wore on, the extremes in our assessments were disconcerting, though I think more for me than for the students. They seemed to adjust their work and response expectations to the professor of the moment. I was uncomfortable, though, because I felt Natalie and I were sending two totally opposite messages.

Our opposed grading approaches showed up quickly in our teaching styles as well. When I became the major facilitator, I set up the room in a circle and the discussion was dialogical. I posed questions that stimulated personal discussions and connections to the issues at hand. While my sessions were interactive, Natalie adopted a lecture format and even noted once, "I'm not Nina, so forget about all this personal sharing!" To make a long story a little shorter, this experience forced me to stop and reflect deeply on the issue of assessment. I began to see that assessment is more than just a part of the educational process; it is the umbrella that spreads over all that we do as educators and as human beings. I had once resisted assessment and tried to avoid the idea. I could do it no longer.

Assessment as a World View

Gradually during this team-teaching experience, I realized that how one assesses students is how one looks at the world. If a teacher sees the world as a place where only some can be successful and others must fail, it will show up in his or her classroom. In this classroom some will get A's, but of course not everyone ("that just wouldn't be fair!"). Only a few can do high-level A work. If a teacher looks at children and sees only deficits and weaknesses, this vision will govern assessment techniques. Students with more deficits will have a harder time earning those A's and children with fewer deficits will have an easier time. The survival of the fittest becomes the philosophical foundation: The most fit get the A's and the rest fall by the wayside. As I write this, I realize that the suffix "-est" is prevalent in the vocabulary of this world view: the best, fittest, smartest, fastest, brightest, neatest. Inherent in these words, of course, is comparison. We compare one student to another, another and another, which is what I mean when I say that one child's success depends on another's failure. For one to be the fittest, at least two others have to be less fit. Those of you who have been graded on a curve can quickly appreciate the subtle unfairness of the comparison. The curve allows for only a certain percentage of A's, B's, C's, D's and F's, and your A depends on how many people below you fail. You know how you felt when you got a 90 on a test and were denied an A because the A quota had already been filled.

Another World View

You've heard my view of assessment in virtually all my letters so far. As you know, in our community every child is successful because success depends on self progress, not on the progress or accomplishments of others. I view all children from a strengths perspective and promote their growth by encouraging written and oral responses. I begin working with the students from where he or she already is. (I do this with my university students too.) Therefore, as you've already seen in the letter on writing, for example, a child's first story is acceptable—no matter what! From this story, purposeful discussion flows and growth appears in subsequent pieces. Assessment is, quite simply, the way we observe and measure growth.

Self and Community Assessment

Children in our community receive both my assessments and constant opportunities to assess themselves and each other. Yes, and I consider these evaluations valid, and I accept them. Observe how this type of assessment takes place. Here Jason has just finished presenting his individual social studies project on Jesse Owens. All children applaud and the following interaction begins:

Jason:	Okay. Tell me what you like. Maggie?
Maggie:	I like how much information you had.
Jason:	Why?
Maggie:	Because I learned a lot.
Nina:	Okay. Jason what do you get for deadline?
Jason:	"A" because I met the deadline.
Nina:	What's the next grade? Eileen?
Eileen:	Content.
Nina:	Good, and what does content mean? Tony?
Tony:	It means the amount of information.
Nina:	Good, and what do you think Jason should get for amount of information? Remember you need to also think about the last project Jason did. What was your last one, Jason?
Jason:	Um, oh yeah, my autobiography.
Nina:	Okay, Jason, pick someone for advice on your content grade.

Jason: Alex?

Alex: I think you should get an A because you have a lot more information than your last one.

Nina: Do you agree, Jason?

Jason: Yeah, I think I did a lot more work on this.

Nina: I agree. It seems like you used a lot of references. Which did you use?

Jason: Two books and I asked my father, too.

Nina: Good, now what's the next grade?

Kama: Oral presentation.

Jason: Joanne?

Joanne: I think you should get a B in oral presentation because I couldn't hear you in the beginning.

Nina: But did he improve as he continued reading?

Joanne: Yes.

Nina: So what do you think, then? Did he end up doing a good job?

Joanne: Yes. Then I guess he should get an A.

Nina: What do you think, Jason? Do you agree?

Jason: Yeah, I think I got better from last time too.

Nina: OK, next grade is product. What do you think you deserve, Jason?

Jason: Well, I think I should get a C because it wasn't my best handwriting and also it's a little wrinkled.

Nina: I agree. So what area do you need to improve on when you do your next presentation?

Jason: My product.

Nina: And how will you do that?

Jason: Well, maybe I can put the papers in a folder and also write slower so my handwriting is better.

Nina: Good ideas. Also maybe if you make sure you give yourself enough time so you don't have to rush. Thank you, Jason. We've really learned a lot about Jesse Owens. Let's all give Jason another hand.

Those unfamiliar with this kind of self- and collective assessment often assume that the children will automatically give themselves A's. They base this assumption on the traditional classroom where A's are precious commodities and there aren't enough to go around. In my classroom, though, A's can go to everyone if they deserve it—that is, if self-improvement is evident. I would be pleased if all my children get A's. These A's signify that my students have tried as hard as they could at that particular time. If all my children try their best, they all deserve A's! I've said before, there are no invisible standards of perfection for all children to meet. My definitions are broad; I work from where each student begins, and each student pushes ahead and progresses successfully in his or her own individual way. This approach to assessment, as with all other aspects of our classroom, fosters a safe and nurturing atmosphere. I intend to discuss self- and collective assessment within the context of this safety.

Could the conversation with Jason you just read have taken place the first day of school? When you think about it, Jason is in a vulnerable situation. The community is judging his personal work in an honest and open way. The children have learned how to respond positively and critically because they have had opportunities to practice these interactions across the curriculum. They had the time to build trust and they know they are safe and respected. This security allows them to feel confident and secure enough to take risks and grow. This takes time, and no, such a conversation could probably not occur in a classroom filled with children accustomed to competitive assessment.

A lot of teachers assume that an interaction like this could never occur, and they cite an inherent "cruelty" in children, a tendency to cut each other down. I hear this story often, and I understand it. A competitive environment subtly encourages and reinforces this cruelty. In fact, a child can only be cruel in an environment where some must fail for others to succeed. But once these same children learn they are valued for who they are and not compared to others, they are ready for critical conversations that support individual community and growth. These students help each other and challenge themselves to do their best, and they are usually hard on themselves. Jason gave himself a C for product because he knew he deserved a C. He had practice evaluating himself critically and honestly. He accepted his C for these other reasons as well:

1. Jason knew what was expected of him,
2. Jason was himself part of the decision, and
3. Jason received evaluations in a number of other areas too, so that while C might have been a bit low, he had a number of other grades that reflected the strengths of his project.

Another question I frequently hear is, "If you don't agree with the grade the child decides on, what do you do?" As part of the community, I do have just as much right to offer my opinions. If, for example, a child decides she should get an A for her information and I disagree, this typical conversation might follow:

Nina: Why do you think you deserve an A, Mari?
Mari: Well compared to my other project I think I have more information.
Nina: Okay. How many references did you use for this one?
Mari: One. One book.
Nina: And your last one was the one on immigration?
Mari: Yeah, I think I had two books and I interviewed my grandmother.
Nina: So you had more last time, so now what do you think? Did you improve from last time?
Mari: Well not really. I guess I should get a B.
Nina: Yes, a B sounds right. Next time just make sure you add a few more references. This way it will be easier for you to get more information. Let's talk about what kind of references we can use. Raise your hand and tell me what references you use.
Derek: Interviews.

Liz: Books.
Jon: TV shows.
Tracie: Movies.
Dawn: Songs.
Nina: Good, now make sure for your next presentations you use more than the amount you've used before.

This conversation shows me facilitating a grade change and the student agreeing with me. At times, too, a student defends his or her grade so passionately I become convinced that the chosen grade is valid:

Nina: Mel, tell me why you believe you deserve an A for your product.
Mel: Well, I tried my hardest and I took my time with my handwriting.
Nina: So that is your best handwriting?
Mel: Yep. I even did it over two times.
Nina: Did you try harder on this project compared to the last one?
Mel: Yes! I was up until nine last night finishing it.
Nina: Well, you are the one who knows best whether you tried your hardest. You must be proud that you've tried so hard. Congratulations!

If it were totally up to me, I would not assign letter grades. But because the system I teach in requires one or two grades a week in each subject, I had to adjust some of what I do for assessment. Notice, though, I did not adjust my philosophy or allow the system's edicts to undermine my beliefs about community and success. I adjusted the assessment techniques so that they corresponded to my view of the world. Actually, it gets to be kind of fun. I play around and try to squeeze as many grades as I can from one piece of work.

How Do I Derive My Grades?

Reading

The Reading Log: Children keep a log (a notebook) to respond to their reading. In this log, they write about their feelings, favorite characters, what they would change, and so forth. As a matter of fact, they often use team reading questions to guide their reflections in this log. I respond to these logs in written form and orally as I make connections with the student and facilitate continued reflection. When children make an entry they receive a grade. I can also assign a grade on fluency (length) from this log, measuring it by the length of previous entries.

Poetry: I can easily pull an oral grade from poetry based on choral reading of poems together with the whole community. I also can get a memorization grade for individual poems or a set of poems. Since we memorize poetry for a meaningful purpose, a recital, all children memorize the poems. I could also derive a number of grades from the actual performance of the recital. It's worth many grades since the children devote an incredible amount of time and work to this aspect of our community.

Drama: Grades that are pulled from poetry can also come from whatever drama production we happen to be working on.

Discussion: I can pull a participation grade from full-class and team reading discussions. For example, if all team members work on a task during team reading that day, they all receive an A.

Silent Reading: If individuals have successfully participated in silent reading they also receive A's for silent reading that day. (Of course, self-assessment is involved here as I ask many times, "What grade do you think you deserve in silent reading? Team reading? Why?")

Writing

Fluency: I examine drafts over time to note fluency progress. Children receive A's if increased fluency is evident.

Editing: I examine edited drafts and derive grades from the presence of certain conventions and skills.

Handwriting: I evaluate the children's handwriting in their final copy.

Oral Development: I can derive grades in oral development during sharing and TAG. I give A's according to individual improvement on volume, expression and participation.

Content: I examine content of each child's writing pieces for topic variety, detail, and description.

As you know, these grades come from the children's drafts, publications and class sharing and responses. Any mastery of skills is recorded in the children's writing folders, notebooks, and portfolios.

Content area(s)

Deadline: All children receive A's if they bring in their report on or before the deadline.

Content: Children receive a grade for the amount of information in their report. This is measured in comparison to their previous report.

Oral Presentation: Children receive a grade for expression and oral fluency as they orally present their report to the class.

Product: I examine handwriting and neatness of final copy to derive a grade for the final product.

Note-taking: I teach children how to take notes on their friends' reports. I assign children grades on fluency measuring the length by previous entries.

As you heard when we discussed Jason's project, decisions about all these grades involve the student, the community and me.

Portfolios Versus Work Folders

Over the last few years I have refined my use of portfolios in the classroom. I previously devoted little time to portfolios because I wanted to avoid traditional assessment, which involves worksheet after worksheet after worksheet. (And after all those worksheets were finished and graded and put in the grade book, there was filing and filing and more filing into various work folders, one for each subject.) It's a wonder a person finds any time for real teaching and learning. I did find some ways to reduce the wasted time, like collecting the worksheets in alphabetical order and letting the children file their own papers (at least they learned alphabetical order within a purposeful context, I suppose). All in all, it was drudgery for me and when portfolio assessment became the rage I, for one, did not jump for joy. I thought, "Great, another folder to worry about!" The thought of trying to organize portfolios discouraged me, and I became hesitant, then resistant. Over time, and with the help of Debbie, one of my student teachers, I began to understand the power of portfolios when used in a respectful and empowering way.

As John Dewey said, the thought behind the action is most important, and I relate this insight directly to portfolio assessment. Most important is the amount of thought behind portfolio use. We can call any folder a portfolio, but it remains one of those work folders filled with worksheets. Let's examine the major differences:

Work Folders

1. Work folders contain pre-made worksheets covering various areas of the curriculum.
2. All paperwork filed is chosen solely by the teacher.
3. All work is uniform—for example, everyone has a Friday spelling test, a reading unit test, a timed addition math test, a handwriting paper copied from the board or from page 12 of the English book.
4. The folders are stored in a cabinet and pulled out for filing, open house, parent and teacher conferences, or administrative examination.
5. Teachers or their aides spend time grading and filing many weekly papers.
6. Papers in the folders are graded and placed there to "prove" the students' report card grades.

Portfolios

1. The material in each portfolio includes various formats including original drawings, writings, photographs, logs, and so forth.
2. Students and teachers are active and equal participants in creating, developing and maintaining each individual portfolio.
3. While some similar work will be part of most students' portfolios—like diary entries and published books—this work is unique to each student.
4. Portfolios are placed for easy and continuous access by the students since the portfolio use is integrated with regular classroom activities.
5. Work is placed in portfolios by teachers, students and other community members on an individual basis and blocks of time for filing are not necessary.
6. The work in the folder shows the student's progress and his or her favorite pieces of work.

Notice the major difference between portfolios and work folders: the roles of the teacher and students. A principle of portfolio use is that the students can choose the work they want to include. Another principle connects to the world view that sees the children's strengths as an important part of teaching, learning and assessment.

Let me explain how I organized portfolio assessment in my third grade classroom last year. First, I asked my student teacher to help me develop a purposeful, organized way to include portfolios. Luckily, her strength lay with organization, one of my weaknesses. So we worked well together. She gathered some checklist-type sheets, and I thought about how best to encourage students to understand the philosophy and purpose of portfolios:

Nina: Today we're going to start developing our portfolios. Raise your hand if you want to tell me what we mean by "portfolios."

Enrique: Folders that we put our work in.

Nina: Yes, they could be folders if we want them to be and they are a place where we keep some of our work in. How do we choose what work goes into our portfolios?

Rea: Well the stuff we get grades on, like our spelling tests and reading units.

Nina: Yes, some teachers might do it like that. But in our class it will be different because you know we do a lot of things in our room that we don't get grades for. What things do we do that we don't really get grades for?

Nick: Our diaries.

Nina: True. What else?

Shana: Writing drafts.

Nina: Yes, others?

Clayton: Our books.

Nina: Yes, and how about our science and social studies logs, poetry and plays? There are really a lot of things we do that we don't get grades for. Raise your hand if you would still like to remember some of these things? Good. I see all of you would, because I know you all love what you do and work really hard at it. So the way we will use our portfolios is to put there the work we want to remember and the work that we think is our best work or just the work that we loved the most! Why do you think it might be important to keep some of the work we've already done?

Oprah: Because we like it and we don't want to throw it away.

Nina: Yes, that's a reason. Others?

Sam: Well, we might want to show our parents.

Nina: Oh, so why would we show our work to them?

Dawn: So that they see how we are doing in school.

Nina: Good point. Now who else should know how you are doing in school?

Kyli: Your grandmother.

Meagan: Your sisters and brothers.

Nina: Who else besides people in your family?

James: You.

Nina: Okay, me, because I'm the teacher and who else? (No response.) Who else should care about your work? Whose work is it? Whose work will be in your portfolio, Derek?

Derek: Mine.

Nina: That's right, your work. Are you proud of the work you do?

Derek: Yes.

Nina: I know you are! Do you want to make sure you are doing your best in school?

Derek: Yes.

Nina: Good. Your portfolios will help you to see how you're doing as the year goes on. It's important that your family knows how you're doing and that I know, too. But it is most important that you feel proud about how you're doing so you will be able to look at your portfolio whenever you want. Raise your hand if you are proud of all the things that you do in our community. Good! You all should be proud and so it is important that the work you put in your portfolio is work that you want to put in. This portfolio will show a little bit of who you are. So Alex, do you think your portfolio will be the exact same as Tiffany's?

Alex: No.

Nina: Why not?

Alex: Because I do different things than Tiffany, like my books are different from hers.

Nina: Exactly. So all of our portfolios will be different because we write different stories, read different books and do different projects. Do you think the work you put in this week will be different from the work you put in next month?

Michael: Yes.

Nina: Why do you think so?

Michael: Because we'll be doing different things.

Nina: True. And do you think you will improve as time goes on? (No response.) Raise your hand if you can tell me what improve means?

Jenny: Like doing more.

Mari: Getting better.

Nina: Yes, and another way we say improvement is "making progress." So our portfolios will be a collection of our favorite work, and they will show how we improve over the year. Let's start thinking about how we want our portfolios to look. Any ideas? (No response.) Well some classrooms use folders, but others use boxes, like shoe boxes or cereal boxes. Raise your hand and tell me what you think.

Notice that this first talk addressed the major principles. Reread the discussion and pick out where these principles emerge. Let's look. We talked about what goes into portfolios and mentioned that portfolio work doesn't have to be graded work and that it can be chosen for many reasons—because it's enjoyable or your favorite, for example. We also talked about the personal importance of portfolios and personal monitoring of progress. We spoke as well about the uniqueness of each portfolio. Also running through the whole discussion notice the pivotal theme of student empowerment. As you heard, I urged the children to be proud of their work and to take ownership of it because it is their work, because they need to care about it, and because they'll want to monitor their own progress. The children also designed their own portfolios, building on those feelings of ownership. On another day the same week, I extend the discussion this way:

Nina: Now that we have our portfolios designed, let's talk about what we will do with them. Raise your hand and tell me what you'll put in your portfolio now.

Allie: My diary, because it's finished.

Nina: Okay. And why would you want to keep your diary?

Mercy: So I could look at it later.

Nina: And why would we want to look at it later? (No response.) Remember what we talked about last time? About progress and improvement? Why do we want to look back on our work sometimes?

Billy: So we can see if we've gotten better.

Nina: Exactly. It helps us see how we've improved. It's like when we do our individual presentations. When we think about what grades we should get, we think about our last project and talk about how we've improved and what we need to work on for next time. That's exactly what we're going to start doing when we work with our portfolios, too. So if you want to evaluate your progress in your diaries, what will you do? (No response.) What do you think "evaluate" means? Okay, let me give you a hint. Let's see, when I look at two books, I take the time to evaluate which one I want to read.

Grace: Like think about which one you want.

Nina: Okay. Any other ideas?

Tom: You have to look through them and decide if you like them.

Nina: That's right. When you evaluate your work, you think about it and decide how you are doing. Another word I like to use is "reflect." Raise your hand if you've heard this word before. Good, I see some of you remember! When do you hear me use this word a lot?

Kim: With the university students. (My undergraduate classes learn how to teach language arts by coming into my elementary classroom once a week and learning with the children.)

Nina: That's right! I'm always asking them to reflect on their readings! Now we can use this word. We always need to reflect on our work and how we are progressing. Now how are we going to evaluate our progress in our diaries? Remember how we do our individual presentations.

Jason: We look back on our first days of writing and see if we wrote more on the next days.

Nina: Excellent! That's right, you look at how much you've written before and compare it to how much you write now, and if it's more than before, you have improved. Remember we talked about the word we use for the amount of writing you do. Raise your hand if you remember it. Sean?

Sean: "Fluency."

Nina: That's right. We evaluate our fluency when we look at our diary entries. Excellent! What grade does that you remind you of in individual projects? Aurora?

Aurora: Amount of information

Nina: Yes, that's what I was thinking of too. Now what if you look at your diary and you notice you haven't really improved in fluency. What can you do? (No response.) Think about it. If don't have a lot of information in one project, what will you work on for the next project?

Zack: Putting in more information

Nina: Exactly. Now if you haven't improved in fluency in your diary, what will you work on for next week?

Angie: Writing longer entries.

Nina: Good. When we decide to work on something so that we improve, we call them our "goals." For example, one of my goals for this week is to finish this book I'm reading. What can I do to help myself finish and meet my goal?

Ernie: Read every day.

Nina: Okay. Any other ideas?

Max: Read for a long time every day.

Nina: Thanks. What I'm trying to do is make sure I have this book with me all the time, and whenever I am waiting—like on line at the store—or whenever we do silent reading, I make sure I read. Another thing I'm trying to do is read at least a few pages right before I go to sleep. Now, if your goal is to become more fluent in your diary entries, what are some things you could do to meet this goal?

Eileen: Think about what you're going to write the night before.

Mike: The minute you come in the morning start writing.

Nina: Oh yes, so you'll have more time. Others?

Natalie: Take your diary to lunch if you didn't write enough in the morning.

Nina: Great! So there are lots of things we can do to meet our goals? What if we can't think of some of these things? What can we do?

Barney: Ask a friend.

Nina: Exactly just like in reading and writing, when we work with our portfolios, our friends and teachers can help us. When a friend looks at your portfolio or you look at a friend's, what would be a good way to respond to the work? (No response.) Well, how do we respond to our friend's writing?

Marilyn: TAG.

Nina: Yes, let's use TAG when we look at our portfolios. If you are looking at it by yourself, the first thing you do is think about what you like about the work, then ask yourself questions about your work, then think about ideas and goals you need to work on for your future work. If you're looking over your portfolio with a friend, then you do it exactly the way we share our other work: Tell what you like, ask your friend questions and give him or her ideas. Now what questions could you ask about the portfolios?

David: Why did they choose the work they chose?

Nina: Good! Oh wait. What can I do with these questions? Like with the questions we ask in team reading?

Myrna: Put them on a chart.

Nina: Yes, that's what I was thinking. Let me write them on the board quickly and then later I'll write them on a chart. So another question we can ask?

Adam: What is your favorite work?

Nina: Good and what do we ask after all our questions?

Debbie:	Why?
Nina:	Yes, why is it your favorite work? Other questions?
Teddy:	What are you going to put in next time?
Nina:	Yes, and why. Others? (No response.) What are we setting for ourselves to improve? What's that word I used when we talked about fluency and me finishing my book?
Marsha:	"Goals."
Nina:	Yes, that's a very important question: What will your goals be for next week? or What do you want to improve on? Another important question would be, Did you meet your goals from last week? What happens if we don't meet all the goals we set? Do we just forget about them? (No response.) Well what happens if I don't finish my book by the end of the week? Am I going to get upset and forget about it, or do you think I will keep trying to read it?
Mike:	You will keep trying to finish it.
Nina:	That's right, I'll just keep the same goal until I meet my goal. So if you don't meet all the goals you set in one week what will you do?
Marilyn:	Put the same goal for the next week.
Nina:	True. Kind of like our spelling tests. If we get the word wrong, we just put in on our list for next week. Now what ideas can we give our friends about the work in their portfolios? (No response.) Remember some of the ideas we had when we talked about working on fluency?
Derek:	We can give them ideas about what they can do to help them meet their goals.
Nina:	Good! We can also give them ideas about what goals they can set, too. And that's what we're going to do right now. I want you to look through your portfolios and start deciding what goals you will be working on. Now how are you going to remember the goals?
Natalie:	Write them down.
Nina:	Yes, that's a good idea. Get out a piece of paper so that you can write your goals down. Look through your portfolios carefully by yourself for a little while and after about five minutes if you want to you can ask for help or help one of your classmates. Now, does spelling matter when you write these goals?
Zack:	No.
Nina:	That's right. It's just for you to remember, as long as you can read it. I'll be working on some of my goals too and then in five minutes I'll come around and see how you all are doing. Let's begin.

The children wrote three or four goals each on a separate strip of paper and left them either in their portfolio or on their desks so they had easy access to them. During the next portfolio session they reflected on whether they had met their goals, and if so, they attached a piece of work that illustrates this completed goal. For example, if one goal was to write a draft in a different genre, this draft (or a copy of it if the child was still at work on it) was attached and placed in the portfolio. If goals go unmet, my children carry them over until they can successfully complete them. The goals are usually appropriate since the children are involved in their formation, but if a goal seems inappropriate, I will facilitate its revision in the same way I help a child evaluate whether spelling words are too easy or too difficult:

Nina:	Sandy, how long have you been working on this goal?
Sandy:	I think about three weeks.
Nina:	That's what I thought. So what's happening? Are you having a hard time with it?
Sandy:	Well, I've been trying to write a poem, but every time I start I can't finish it. It always ends up being more of a story.
Nina:	Oh, so do you really like to write poetry?
Sandy:	I guess not really.
Nina:	Well why don't you try another genre that you might like better and maybe another time during the year, poetry will become easier for you to write.

(If Sandy said she really liked poetry and still wanted to try to write poetry, I probably would have suggested that she coauthor a poem with someone who has written poetry before.)

You've noticed, of course, that we had a thorough discussion about portfolios before the children took possession of them. These discussions consume time but in a critically literate classroom they are essential. We discuss, examine and develop within community conversations all that we do and plan to do.These discussions allow all children to be influential participants actively shaping their environment. Traditional teachers supply more answers, write quick directions on the board, specify their lessons and save time this way. In my classroom, as you know, we devote much time to questioning students to facilitate personal and community connections to the issues at hand. For example, to help make the idea of the portfolio more concrete, I connected the idea to project and spelling tests. I also introduced some new vocabulary as the words came naturally into use within the activity at hand. Isolated vocabulary drills on "fluency," "reflecting," "evaluation," and "goals," never occurred since the students continually use these words as they engage in purposeful work. I, myself, use these words frequently as I question and facilitate individual portfolio conversations.

For a moment now, let's look at this conversation within the context of my entire curriculum. Do you see how everything we talked about in relation to portfolios connects to literacy interactions? I introduced portfolio vocabulary the same way I introduce the vocabulary of authors: while children are involved in authentic writing. Notice, too, that the patterned way we respond to written work

(TAG), be it our narrative drafts or an individual presentation, also guides responses to portfolios. I, the teacher, include myself in the community "we" as I set personal goals and share them with the students. Choice and power are evident here as they are in all other aspects of our community. Children choose the work they reflect upon and choose the goals they will work toward within a community of learners that will encourage the choice and facilitate the growth.

Sample Literacy Goals

Write more in my diary.
Make sure I write every day in my diary.
Write more in my reading log.
Write more for my homework.
Write longer stories.
Put more details in my stories.
Put more dialogue in my stories.
Make sure I have a setting in my stories.
Read a new genre.
Write in a new genre.
Pick a book I really like.
Coauthor something with someone.
Write a story by myself.
Help others more during writing.
Participate more in team reading.
Participate more when the teacher asks questions.
Participate more during TAG.
Sign up to share more.
Talk louder when I share my stories and during individual presentations.
Study my poetry every night.
Study my script every night.
Pick easier words for spelling.
Pick harder words during spelling.
Pick words that I really want and need to learn how to spell.

Sample of General Community Goals

Help people on my team stay focused.
Help people on line follow the rules.
Ask for help to follow the rules.
Ask for help when I need it.
Help others when they ask me.

Sample Positive Comments—T—Tell What You Like

I like the picture of the octopus you made and put up when we were talking about the ocean 'cause it looks really cool!

I like how you met all your goals last week 'cause it shows you concentrated.

I like how you decorated the outside of your portfolio because it looks really cool!

I like how you wrote that your favorite book is *Shiloh* because it's mine too.

I like that you put your immigration project in your portfolio cause you had a lot of information.

Sample A—Ask Questions

What goals will you choose for next time? Why?

Did you complete the goals you set last time? How?

Why did you choose this poem, story, presentation to put in your portfolio?

What is your favorite piece of work? Why?

What do you want to improve on? Why?

Sample G—Give Ideas

Maybe next time you could coauthor because you always write stories by yourself.

Maybe you could work on writing some solo stories because you always do a lot of coauthoring.

I think you should put that story about the monsters in here, because it was one of your best!

Maybe you could put your book in our library so we can all read it.

You could add more detail so we will know more about your characters.

You could add talking to your story so that it's longer.

Instead of saying "he said" or "she said" all the time, you could write "he hollered" or "she cried."

Spelling

For some reason spelling has become an obsession in our traditional educational structure. I remember tears spilled over failed spelling tests and the Thursday night study sessions as frustrated family members quizzed the youngster about to face that dreaded Friday test. My brother went through it all. I remember my mother sitting at the kitchen table with him after dinner. As I finished the dishes, my mother repeated the words over and over, forced him to write them all ten times, then repeated them again, her voice becoming louder and louder. My brother would start to cry. Sometimes my mother cried too. I held my breath praying my brother would finally get the words right and it would all end!

I happened to be good at spelling memorization, so I saved my tears for long division. I realize that nowadays I almost never use long division. Incredible! Was it worth all the suffering? Remembering my brother, I ask this question about spelling, too. My brother is a songwriter and musician now, and I suppose if he has a hard time spelling a word he asks someone or uses the spell check on his word processing program. If I ever have to do a long-division problem, I use a calculator.

Why do you think so many educators still worship the sacred Friday spelling test? Well, when you think about it, the spelling test symbolizes all traditional education holds dear: There is one standard to meet, a child's success or failure can easily be measured against this objective standard, and the words are all decontextualized and isolated. Aren't these elements more or less characteristic of all activities in a traditional classroom? As I'm sure you've already guessed, I resisted implementing such a spelling program and over the years adapted the way we learn to spell so that my philosophical and pedagogical beliefs support it.

In my first year of elementary school teaching in a second grade, I remember the brand new spelling books each child received. The school had just ordered them from a publishing company that advertised the realistic sentences. Each unit had ten words on the first page. The subsequent pages offered fill-in-the-blank sentences that sounded a lot like the same old boring sentences to me: "The bear was brown." At first I tried using these books in a traditional way, assigning the unit on Monday so that children could prepare for their spelling test on Friday. I also assigned the traditional homework: write the words five or ten times, write a sentence for each word.

Though I never could, however, bring myself to assign "Write a story using all ten spelling words." Have you ever tried to write a coherent story with ten unrelated words? How sad to waste time and build frustration trying to complete such a ridiculous assignment! Just thinking about it infuriates me! Anyway, I resisted this traditional assignment and quickly discarded the other spelling book techniques as well. After my first Friday spelling test, I realized I needed to reconsider what I was doing. Was tradition worth having children feel poorly about themselves as they failed these tests? Didn't their failure negate the positive and respectful community that I wanted so much to help develop and facilitate? I redesigned my spelling program.

A Redesigned Spelling Program

Since I had to use the expensive new spelling books, I contrived to include them in my adaptation. I decided to allow the children to use the books in their own way and at their own speed. This simple adjustment allowed me to remain true to what I really believe is right for children and education. They retained a certain amount of choice and all of them could be successful.

Four Variations on a Spelling Book Theme

1. Children are allowed to study a unit for as long as they need to.
2. Children are allowed to study more than one unit at a time.
3. Spelling tests are given throughout the week whenever a child thinks he or she is ready.
4. During the school day at a special time, the children help each other study and give each other practice spelling tests.

For example, one day I might say this:

Nina: Okay, anybody who's ready for the unit 2 spelling test come up with your paper and pencil. (The children come to a conference table and I give them the test. One, two or ten children might take the test. When all are finished, I marked them on the spot as I talk to each child about his or her individual test.) Good, Debbie you got eight right. Now you need to practice these two. I'll give another test tomorrow or if you find the time to study today remind me and I'll try and give you one before we go home.

Sometimes, I give the whole test over again to the child, or if I'm certain she really knew the eight words, I test her only on the two she got wrong. When she spells them correctly, she moves to the next unit. I also vary the way I give the test, and if the children want to I let them spell orally. I found that many students wanted to complete two and three units at a time, so I adjusted the testing to accommodate their eagerness by calling more than one unit at a time: "Whoever is ready to take units 6 and 7 please come up."

It fascinated me to see the children eat this up. They became spelling fiends who wanted to zip through these units as fast as possible. And did they ever! By January most of the class had completed the book and so had officially mastered the second-grade curriculum in spelling! This mastery, meanwhile, gave me more time to devote to what I thought was more important: Real writing and reading. Moreover, I had no spelling grades to worry about for the rest of the year. Each unit grade was put in the weekly designated place in the grade book, and by January, all the places for the year was filled. The only trouble was my children all wanted to go on to the third grade spelling book. At this point, determined to be free of spelling in the traditional sense, I allowed them to give each other the tests.

As I began to refine my writing program, traditional spelling instruction—even with my variations—became more and more a disturbing and unnatural part of my community. Because I teach everything and the children carry out all their activities within a purposeful and contextualized framework, isolated and impersonal spelling words just don't fit in. Therefore, I now address spelling during writing in a meaningful way. As you've already read in the letter on the writers' workshop, all writing skills receive attention when they are most important. Accordingly, I address spelling as the children edit their drafts for publication. This helps the children see when and why spelling is important. Really, if it were up to me, I would eliminate any kind of spelling test. As we saw in the letter on writing, when children write consistently and purposefully, they develop spelling skills naturally. Just look at a kindergarten or a first grade child's writing over time and you will see spelling stages emerge. The invented spelling in a true writers' workshop actually promotes this spelling progression. Therefore, in my view, examining drafts over time is the most natural and meaningful way to assess spelling.

These past few years, however, I have been team teaching a third-grade public school class with another teacher, Faye Slater. When I began working with Faye, I saw she already had an individualized spelling program in place. When she began to explain it to me it sounded so complicated I wondered whether it was worth the time I would rather devote, as usual, to real writing and reading. Faye's excitement, though, kept me watching and reflecting on her program. Once I saw how she implemented it, I compromised just a little while acknowledging it created none of the dissonance a traditional model would create in our community.

Individualized Spelling

As you read the following nine guidelines for individualized spelling, think about how they correspond with the basic tenets of a critically conscious classroom:

1. The children pick their own weekly spelling words; the number may vary with age, but all children in the same community receive the same number of words.
2. The children choose their words from one of their edited drafts using words that needed to be corrected, from personal reading, from class poetry or from presentations.
3. The children write their spelling words in their spelling log and in their homework notebook.
4. The spelling tests are given at the same time in pairs. Partners read spelling logs together to ensure that they can read each other's words.
5. One partner stands behind the other with the partner's spelling log and gives the spelling test.

6. The children switch places so the other child receives a test. The children are not permitted to erase during test.

7. An adult circulates around the room correcting finished tests.

8. Words spelled incorrectly or erased are placed on next week's spelling list.

9. The children pick new words from edited drafts, reading, class poetry and presentations for next week's spelling test and copy them into spelling log and homework notebook.

Notice where in individualized spelling the spelling words come from. They come from whole, purposeful and personally meaningful messages. This feature complements my effort to connect personally and contextualize all our work. Here, too, we focus on spelling when it is naturally important, in edited copy. In addition, the children begin to appreciate spelling words for the beauty of their sound and the interest of their meanings. Here's how our students describe the program and how they decide what words to choose:

Nina:	Let's come together as a class and review the way we do our spelling. We're going to use this video to show the university students. What do we do first?
Anais:	Make sure the person giving you the test knows how to read your words.
Nina:	Okay, but even before that.
Adri:	Study.
Nina:	Oh, of course! In this class we study every day of our lives! (laughter) Now after we study, what do we do when we get ready for our test?
Guari:	Get a little piece of paper and put our names on it. (Precut paper is always available for spelling tests. The paper is small so the test can fit into a letter-sized envelope stapled to the back of each child's spelling log.)
Nina:	Good. The next thing?
Alex:	Read over spelling words with your partner to make sure they can read your words and you can read theirs.
Nina:	Okay and then what?
Erica:	Stand behind your partner and whisper their words in their ear.
Nina:	Good. And who's holding your partner's log?
Erica:	You are because you have to read their words and they have yours.
Nina:	And what happens when you finish giving the spelling test to your partner?
Yve:	Then they give it to you.
Nina:	Next? Then what happens when both of you are finished?
Emma:	Wait to be checked.
Nina:	What do you do while you're waiting?
Sue:	Look for your new words.
Nina:	Where do you get your words?

> Alex: Go to your writing or your personal reading book and pick ten new words.
> Nina: What happens to words you missed?
> Mae: You put them on your new list.
> Nina: That's right, so you can study them some more. And what do you do with the spelling test after it is corrected?
> Doug: Inside the envelope on your spelling log.
> Nina: Right, so you can always see your improvement. One more thing, after I've checked the new words you put in your log, where else do you copy these new words?
> Kit: In your homework notebook.
> Nina: Why are you copying them there, too?
> Joe: So you don't have to bring home your spelling log and you have them with you to study every night.

As the children take their tests I circulate, monitoring and encouraging the children individually. At times I might actually stop the class to share important ideas or news:

> Let's come together as a class for a minute. Guess what? Joey just got his new words yesterday and he only got two wrong! Let's give him a hand! I also want to mention how hard you all are studying. Congratulations!

When both partners are done administering their tests I check them. If I have an aide or student interns, they help me. But even by myself, though, this is a brief process. The children use the time waiting for me to pick their new words, copy them into their homework notebooks, then go right into silent reading. As I check the spelling test, I also check their new words to make sure they are spelled in the standard way before the children study them. Because the words come from personal reading, class poetry, scripts, books we've read aloud, and edited copy of personal writing, they are already spelled in the standard way, and checking the new words is just a matter of scanning.

Materials Needed for Individualized Spelling Program

- Purposeful, contextualized reading, writing, poetry, and scripts, where a child can find standard spelling words
- A spelling log for each child
- An envelope stapled to the spelling log where each child can store spelling tests
- Precut blank paper for spelling tests
- A homework notebook

Teachers often ask me how I monitor the words children choose for individualized spelling. Many assume that children will naturally pick easy words and "take the easy way out." Others wonder what happens if a child continually gets the same words wrong. While these situations might occur frequently in a classroom with a traditional assessment perspective, they don't in my classroom. Why, do you think? And while you're thinking consider this exchange:

Nina: Let's say you know in your heart that you've been studying hard every night—and you know that better than I do—and you still get some words wrong. What do you think you should do for your next spelling test? I'm thinking of a few things.

Ketty: Study harder.

Nina: Okay, and what if you've studied the hardest you could? Another thing?

Elly: Pick easier words.

Nina: Okay. Any other ideas? What else about the words? (No response.)
Think about how we do reading? Do I choose all the books that you read?

Derek: No.

Nina: That's right. Why don't I?

Jo: Because you want us to read books that we like.

Nina: Exactly. We read more when we are reading what we want to read. Now how can we relate this idea to our spelling words? (No response.) Pick words that what?

Jason: That you like!

Nina: Yes! Why would you want to pick boring words to spell? Now tell me some of the words you've picked. Anais?

Anais: "Dramatically."

Nina: Why did you choose that word?

Anais: It's kind of hard.

Nina: Good! So you want to challenge yourself. Raise your hand if you like to challenge yourself. Good! When we challenge ourselves we help ourselves grow. What does "dramatic" mean?

Mario: Like when you say "Oh, my gosh I got it wrong!"

Nina: Good. Like when you exaggerate a little. Like when you say "Oh, I have a terrible stomach ache!!" Like an actress. Raise your hand if you're a good actress. (Most girls raise their hands.) Eileen, you're a good actress!! Remember how dramatic you were in "Snow White?" Now, raise your hand if you're a good actor. (All boys raise their hands.)
Good! If you say things dramatically, you are a good actress or actor.
Excellent word, Anais! Do you love that word?

Anais: Yes.

Nina: Good, so make sure you pick words you love and want to learn. And what happens if you see that you are getting A's on your spelling tests without even studying at all. What could that mean?

Pat: That the words are too easy.

Nina: Probably. What's the use of trying to spell words you already know? Would you be challenging yourself if you picked words that were too easy?

Henry: No.

Nina: But I know you all challenge yourself in this class because you all love to learn. Let's hear some of the new words you've chosen.

You will be amazed at some of the words the children in this type of classroom pick. Here are a few from the third grade class I've been describing:

> vulnerable
> amazing
> megaton
> kryptonite
> mutant
> reflective
> radioactive

As you can probably tell these words come from material many children identify with. But why else do these children naturally challenge themselves? Why aren't they picking easy words? Think about their classroom community. Do they feel safe there? Do they feel accepted? Yes, as you've seen throughout our discussion, this classroom is designed so that all children feel secure and successful. This confidence nurtures a child's natural curiosity and desire to learn. Children eagerly take the risks that are so much a part of continued growth. With this type of spelling children receive recognition for their choice of real and challenging words. Nor is it a big deal if they choose a challenging word and miss it on the spelling test. They know they will have a chance to try again. Indeed, our spelling becomes exciting and challenging as all other aspects of our literacy program support it. As you know, we even connect children's words to other events in the classroom and transform spelling into a contextualized vocabulary lesson personally meaningful to our whole community of active authors, readers, playwrights and performers!

Another issue that I'm often asked to address is how I facilitate spelling growth. For example, do I always allow children complete choice in spelling? Yes, I do—just as I allow it in reading and writing. That doesn't mean, though, that I withhold suggestions to the full class or individual students. During editing I might suggest spelling words by noting that a student seems to like a particular word or uses it frequently in personal writing. I might suggest that a student change a spelling word if I see it has been on a spelling test for a long time, or if I see a ridiculously easy word (which happens only rarely). As you saw in the last discussion, if a word is too difficult, a decision to change it is appropriate. Remember, as in all other aspects of the community, we are here to make sure all children are both successful and challenged. Also, I often question a student about his or her personal connection to the chosen words. As with everything else, I consistently ask, "Why did you choose that word?" Children should have a personal and strong personal reason for every word they choose!

Now, let me ask you another question: Do you think I would vary the number of spelling words within the same classroom or would I require the same number of words for every child in the classroom? A few more questions may give you some hints: What message would I be sending if everyone had a different number of words to learn for each test? What if I said, "Oh Jose, you pick five spelling words and Anais, you pick ten and Eileen, you pick fifteen." What messages about expectations am I sending to these three students? How might Jose feel? How might Eileen feel? Are these appropriate feelings in my cooperative classroom?

Put yourself in Jose's position. While you might think that Jose will be delighted to get only five spelling words, when you think about it seriously you'll come to a different view. In effect, Jose is hearing that he is not competent enough to handle the work Anais and Eileen handle. Jose receives a clear message that I expect less of him. Meanwhile, Anais and Eileen hear that they are both competent and better than Jose. This message, of course, runs completely contrary to all my beliefs about community classrooms. Indeed, this one technique could quickly unravel my whole philosophical and pedagogical fabric.

I can hear some of you saying, "Wait a minute, Nina. Aren't we supposed to be meeting the needs of all our students? Adjusting the words is just one way to do this. Maybe not all children can handle the same number of words."

Well, there are different ways to meet the needs of each child, and we should think carefully about the ways we chose so that they neither condescend nor discourage. Think about my spelling program: While all the children have the same number of words all their personal needs are also being met. What have I built into individualized spelling (and for that matter, into everything we do) that allows this to happen? The first is choice! When students choose their words, as you've seen, they usually meet their needs! Also, because they can carry words over to subsequent tests, the time for mastery is flexible and personalized. As I write this, I realize that my spelling program is more than just "individualized," it is "personalized." Maybe I'll start calling it *Personalized Spelling*! Which do you prefer? Why? (You're not going to get away without me asking Why!)

More Reflections

So what do you think this about this radical approach to spelling instruction? Do you think you can withstand the pressure of doing what everybody else does and become a transformative educator? Or will you maintain the status quo and succumb to the Friday testing ritual? You might not be sure of the answer now, but you should reflect on the question and formulate your answer. The answer to this question will influence everything else you do in education. As I said earlier, the way you assess reflects the way you look at the world and your philosophy about life and learning. The answer to this question will determine whether all your children feel safe, successful and worthy or if only some feel this way. How will your children feel?

Keep strong!

Nina

Nina

LETTER #10
THE NATURE OF INSTRUCTION:
RETHINKING OBJECTIVES, PROCEDURES,
AND EVALUATION

> *Suggesting that the curriculum be teacher-centered is in fact a departure from conventional schooling. When teaching in conventional classrooms is carefully examined, one actually finds teachers, not at the center of the elementary curriculum, but on its edge along with the children. Putting teachers at the core of the curriculum implies that they have substantive ideas upon which to base their curriculum (are thoughtful, knowledgeable, and curious people in their own right) and that they have the talents to stimulate children's thinking and desire to learn, given proper support.*
>
> *(Goodman, 1992, p. 129)*

Hi Everyone!

It's an interesting quote, isn't it. When I first read it I was a bit startled. I had always assumed that when I said "child-centered," I was describing a democratic, choice-driven community. I never thought of myself as somehow at the center of that community. But of course when I step back and reflect it makes perfect sense. In a conventional classroom, teachers are handed series of books along with manuals and worksheets and make sure to remain on the path the publishers lay out for them. These manuals contain scripts that spell out exactly what the teacher needs to say and even presume to predict the student responses. When you think about it, it's really easy to do since these manuals direct teachers to ask questions that have only one right answer.

Sometimes to add a little variety in a teacher's life (or maybe just to increase their royalties), publishers offer nice organized boxes with little task cards and dividers so that all that one need do is pull it out and read the card! Incredible, don't you think? With some programs a teacher need never open a book! How do you feel about this? Did you come into teacher education just to follow instructions? You know, many who pass through traditional teacher training programs have never had an opportunity to discuss this issue. Too many of us have gone through programs that just distribute recipes to follow no matter what type of community we find ourselves part of.

If recipes are all that you had, you have yet to get a chance to think about who you are as an educator. So take the time now. Really! Right now, sit back and think! Do you want merely to be told what to do—a faithful obedient bureaucrat of the system? Or do you want, in Giroux's expression, to be an "an intellectual professional?" Sound familiar? It should. I put this question back in my second letter: "Will you maintain the status quo or will you begin the transformation of society within your classroom community?"

I hope some of the conventional teacher materials you've seen actually insult you. How dare anyone presume that you and I are unable to hold a meaningful conversation with our students. Even as I write this I become more infuriated. I think that we allow publishing companies to drive our curriculum. Indeed, our conventional classrooms are neither child-centered nor teacher centered; they are publisher-centered. Maybe you don't feel as angry as I do, yet. But as you grow stronger in your philosophical beliefs and more confident in your abilities as an intellectual professional, you will be as disgusted as I am.

We cannot assume, of course, that a few "choice recipes" will be appropriate for all of our classroom communities. Are human beings really that simple? Of course not. We are all complex individuals who grow and develop constantly within the various contexts—family, friends, school, society—that we are connected to. How could one objective, one procedure, one form of evaluation fit all? It's absurd! Since human beings involve themselves in a process of teaching and learning that is as complex as we are ourselves, to break up learning into isolated pieces is to destroy the process itself.

Does all this sound familiar? Remember Vygotsky's H_2O analogy to language? "When one approaches the problem of thinking and speech by decomposing it into its elements, one adopts the strategy of the man who resorts to the decomposition of water into hydrogen and oxygen in his search for a scientific explanation of the characteristics of water, its capacity to extinguish fire. ...This man will discover, to his chagrin, that hydrogen burns and oxygen sustains combustion. He will never succeed in explaining the characteristics of the whole by analyzing the characteristics of its elements."(qtd. In Moll, 1990, p. 6) Same thing here, don't you think? Breaking up the process of learning into minute objectives, rote procedures, and conventional types of assessment elevates activities that ask for mere memorization and recall, not learning at all.

Since you've already read discussions of literacy throughout these letters, I know you all can predict how I plan. Do you think I would limit my children to one or two literacy objectives a week? Do you think I would break up what we discuss in our community into pieces to fit the traditional planning format? If I were forced to, I could write my plans out on paper, but then I would go far beyond what was written in my plan books. After all, who is the driving force behind my curriculum, the publishing companies or the community? The community, of course; therefore, I base all my planning decisions on what we all need for continued success and growth as individuals within a common community. I make these decisions within the context of the classroom—that is, all my lessons are contextualized.

Contextualization

Contextualized instruction is the only way to discuss the skills necessary for the work at hand. All the transcripts of my classroom discussions projects involve contextualization. All lessons, all discussions are derived from classroom activities and work. The framework from which we work is the community itself, not a teacher's manual or a box of cards. Instructional plans emerge from this foundation. For some people the word "emerge" evokes a vision of haphazard instruction that is loose and chaotic. But as you know, this is not true. While I am certainly flexible, my instruction is a lot less open than some might think. In fact, it is quite structured and systematic since our community is engaged in the common work of writing, reading, talking, thinking, sharing, teaching, learning and growing. What emerges from all this work are discussions about conventions and skills that all people engaged in purposeful literacy need to use and develop.

In the school district where I have worked most of my life, we are now being encouraged to integrate the curriculum as much as possible. In other words, we are urged to connect social studies, science, math, writing and reading. This is fine with me. I love to connect. It's fun, it allows you to be creative, and it saves transition time—that wasted time when students and teachers rummage aimlessly through their desks, changing from one activity to another. Every year I try to integrate more and more so that one day I'll have a seamless curriculum where all activities flow into and out of each other. Of course, first and foremost, all major decisions must flow from the lives, interests, desires, strengths and needs of the children. As you know, choice allows me to do this. The children's choices of topics, reading materials and modes of interaction drive our planning.

I leave my topics broad to accommodate all learners in the classroom, and while some might think "She must have a hundred little groups if everyone is working at different places," I don't. I always present my skills lessons to the entire community at the same time. I base my lessons on the topics already planned as well as on what emerges from the work at hand. If, for example, some of our authors want to know how to use quotation marks, I'll write it in my plans and make sure I address this skill in relation to the children's work. Do you think I just get up and start talking about quotation marks on Monday at 8:30 in the morning? Wouldn't this behavior run counter to my belief in contextualization? What I do before discussing this topic is make sure to find a connection in someone's writing or reading. It's best to connect to something I noticed yesterday or earlier today. If I fail to locate a certain topic or skill use in any child's work, I defer the discussion because, again, what we talk about must be valuable to our community.

Imagine my children all involved in the writing process. I am circulating around the room looking for some dialogue in a child's draft. I remember I saw some in Henry's draft yesterday and would like to connect his to someone else's work today. I find dialogue in Toni's draft:

Nina: Toni, I see someone is talking in your story. Do you know what we call this?

Toni: Dialogue.

Nina: That's right! How did you know that?

Toni: Well, I remember we talked about it when we were talking about writing our play.

Nina: Oh! So now you are using it! Can I share this with the rest of the class?

Toni: Okay.

Nina: Listen, everyone come together as a class for a minute. (I wait for everyone to listen.) Please make sure the person next to you is ready to listen. Thank you. I wanted to share something from Toni's story.

	(I write Toni's sentence on the board: "Jeremy screamed, 'I'm going to the Discovery Zone!' ") Look at the sentence and tell me what you think we're going to talk about.
Todd:	Maybe exclamation points.
Nina:	Great idea because you see Toni used one at the end of her sentence. What else could we talk about?
Shari:	How she said "screamed."
Nina:	What do you mean?
Shari:	Well, like sometimes we say "she said, he said," but she said "screamed."
Nina:	Oh! That's true! We talked about that the other day! Who remembers when we talked about that? (Most raise their hands.)
	Good! What other words can we use when we don't want to say "said" all the time?
Ruth:	"Yelled."
Mary:	"Shouted."
Michele:	"Exclaimed."
Jeff:	"Whispered."
Nina:	Excellent ideas. These different words make our stories more interesting to read. Toni also used what in her story? (No response.) What is Jeremy doing in this sentence?
Henry:	Talking.
Nina:	That's right, Henry, talking! You had talking in your story yesterday didn't you Henry?
Henry:	Yes.
Nina:	What did your character say?
Henry:	"I like your limo."
Nina:	Who's saying this?
Henry:	Frank.
Nina:	Okay, Can I write your sentence on the board, too?
Henry:	Okay.
Nina:	Thanks. (I write Henry's words on the board. I add "I said" but leave out the quotation marks.)
	Let's all read this together. Ready, go.
All:	I-like-your-limo, I said.
Nina:	Now let's read what Toni's character says. Everyone
All:	I'm going to the Discovery Zone.
Nina:	Okay. Nice expression. Both Henry and Toni have talking in their story. What's another word for that writers use when their characters are talking. (Toni raises her hand.) I see your hand, Toni. Let's give a few more minutes for others to think.
Jarrett:	Like in a movie.
Nina:	Good, you're thinking! Others?
Toni:	Dialogue
Nina:	Good. Dialogue is a word we use for talking. Let's look at Toni and Henry's dialogue again. Does anyone notice

anything?

(No response.) When we write dialogue down we use certain marks that show us what the people are saying. Do you see here where I put the marks for Toni's dialogue. Now let's look at Henry's sentence. Are all these words talking or just some?

Maggie: Just some.

Nina: Which ones?

Maggie: I like your limo.

Nina: Exactly. The person here doesn't say "Frank said," It's just to show who's talking. Where do you think we would put those marks in Henry's sentence? (No response.) Look at Toni's sentence. Maybe that will help you decide. Pedro?

Pedro: Like before and after.

Nina: Good! What's the first word that Henry's character says here?

Jon: I.

Nina: Good. Now what's the last word he says?

Chris: Limo.

Nina: Yes. Now, where should we put the marks? Someone come up and try. (Many raise their hands.) Henry, why don't you pick someone since it's your writing!

Henry: Steve. (Steve places them correctly.)

Nina: Yes, Steve. We put them before the first word the character says and after the last word the character says. Let's give Steve a hand for coming up and trying. Does anyone know what those marks are called?

Eileen: Talking marks?

Nina: Excellent! That's exactly what they are! What writers usually call them is quotation marks. So when you want to use dialogue in your story, who could you go to if you need help?

Alex: Toni.

Nina: Okay. Who else?

Dan: Henry.

Nina: Good. Now, raise your hand if you've already used dialogue in a story. (A number of children raise their hands.) Everyone look around so you can see who you can ask to help you. Now, who is thinking of using dialogue in their next story? (A number of children raise their hands.) Great! It's fun to experiment with new things in our stories. Thanks for listening. Let's all get back to what we were doing.

After writers' workshop, the community begins to go into silent reading. Today I decide to guide this silent reading session a bit:

Nina: What do you think I'm going to ask you to do during silent reading?

	(No response.) Think about it. What have we been talking about today? Oops! I just gave a hint!! *Talking* about? Marla?
Marla:	Dialogue.
Nina:	That's right. So what I want you to do during silent reading is notice whether your author uses dialogue. You may begin silent reading.(After a while, I close silent reading in this way.) Beautiful silent reading, everyone! I could tell everyone was really focused on their books! Let's come together as a class for a minute and hear some examples of dialogue you've found in your reading. Raise your hand if you would like to share what you've found. Bobby?
Bobby:	It's the Grinch. "These stockings," he grinned, "are the first things to go!"
Nina:	Good! Let's write that on the board. (I write it without the quotation marks.) Now what is the first word the Grinch says?
Bobby:	These.
Nina:	Okay. So where do we put the first set of quotation marks? Come up and show us.
Missy:	In front of the word "These." (She notates correctly.)
Nina:	Good and someone else come put up the last set of marks. Missy you pick someone.
Missy:	Aurora.
Aurora:	After the last word "go." (She notates correctly.)
Nina:	Excellent! Let's all give Missy and Aurora a hand for trying. (The community claps as the girls sit down.) Remember only what he *says*. Did he say he grinned?
All:	No.
Nina:	That's right. And here's something we haven't spoken about yet. You see how Dr. Seuss put "he grinned" in between what the Grinch said. Well, because he did that, we need to put two more sets of quotation marks. Watch. See, we put them after "stockings" and then before "are." This way we can tell right away what the character is saying since all the words he says are between quotation marks. Let's all read only what the Grinch says. Ready, go. (I point as the children read)
All:	These stockings are the first to go.
Nina:	Good! You only read the words that are between the quotation marks. Now, let's all get into team reading and I bet you know what I am going to ask you to discuss first. Mario?
Mario:	Dialogue! (Everyone laughs.)
Nina:	Yes—you all can be the teacher! Make sure everyone in your team gets a chance to share the dialogue they found in their personal reading. If we are still in team reading and your team is finished with sharing dialogue, what will you all do?

| Barbara: | Keep talking about your books and asking team reading questions. |
| Nina: | Right. Let's all begin team reading. |

The children scatter around the room and form into teams, and I circulate, monitoring and facilitating conversations. Then I begin to close the team reading session:

Nina:	Okay. Stay in your teams but let's talk as a full class now. I am going to go around to every team so they can share one piece of dialogue they found. I'm going to give you all two minutes to decide which dialogue your team wants to share. Also, you need to decide who will read the dialogue. Ready, go. (Two minutes pass.)
Nina:	Okay, let's begin. Mario's team?
Joan:	She said I want to go home.
Nina:	Did she say, "she said" or just I want to go home? Look and see what words are between the quotation marks.
Joan:	I want to go home.
Nina:	Okay, good. Thank you. Next team?

After each team has a chance to share, the team reading session closes, all the children go to their seats, and I start the common read-aloud book. As I read, I stop periodically to point out examples of dialogue:

Nina:	As I'm reading our next chapter of *Charlotte's Web*, let's see what kind of dialogue E. B. White uses. Does this author usually include a lot of dialogue?
Karen:	Yes, because mostly *everyone* talks!
Nina:	That's for sure. Even the animals talk!! Which is your favorite talking animal?
Daniel:	I like the goose because she says things three times.
Nina:	Good, and I like how you defended your answer and said why you liked the goose. Someone else?
Chris:	I like Charlotte because she called Wilbur a terrific pig!
Nina:	Good, and you defended your answer, too. So let's listen and see who's talking in this chapter. (We bring reading aloud to a close talking about E. B. White's dialogue.) So what did you think about the dialogue in this chapter?
Brad:	I liked it.
Nina:	Why?
Brad:	Because it sounded real. Like when Wilbur said "I just love it here in the barn."
Nina:	That's an excellent reason, Brad. Many authors do use dialogue so that their stories sound more real. It's funny, even though animals don't really talk, in this book E. B. White makes it seem like the most natural thing! Has anyone here

	ever put talking animals in their work? Derek?
Derek:	Remember my third story had my dog Tasha talking?
Nina:	Oh yeah, that's right. What kind of dog is Tasha?
Derek:	A black Lab.
Nina:	I just thought of something. Maybe when you get older you'll read a book called *Animal Farm*. It's by George Orwell. All the animals talk in this book, too! Just like Wilbur, there are talking pigs! Okay. Raise your hand if you are thinking of putting talking animals in your story? Wow! Lots of you! I can't wait to hear what all these animals are going to say! Hey, maybe we can write a play full of talking animals! What do you think?
Class:	Yeah!!
Nina:	Okay, let's think about it and remind me to talk about it some time this week. Now let's get a few individual projects presented today. Raise your hand if you still need a chance to present. (A number of students raise their hands.) Okay. Now what I want you all to do is skim through your project and then raise your hand if you have any examples of dialogue. Why do you think I'm asking you to do this?
Alison:	So that we get more practice with dialogue and so everything is connected.
Nina:	Exactly. Now take about two minutes to skim. When you find an example, raise your hand. Emma?
Emma:	(Stands in front of the class.) Moises is ready. Becca is sitting nicely. (She reads her presentation. When she finishes the class gives her a hand. She chooses children to respond to her work with TAG, just as in writing.)
Mare:	I like how you used dialogue in your presentation because that's what we're talking about now.
Mickey:	Why do you think you said that when you were a baby?
Emma:	Maybe because I didn't say it right since I didn't know how to pronounce it. That's what my grandmother said.
David:	Maybe next time you can put more dialogue in so that there is more detail.
Emma:	Thank you.
Nina:	Let's give Emma a hand. (The community claps as Emma sits down and I hang up her project on the bulletin board.) Before we go to lunch let's decide what we should do for homework. What do you think I'm thinking of?
Michael:	Dialogue! (Everyone laughs.)
Nina:	You people are always reading my mind! Or maybe I'm reading yours! So any suggestions?
Annie:	Write down three examples of dialogue.
Jaime:	Write down three things your mother tells you tonight.
Louise:	Write down some dialogue you hear from TV.

Nina: These ideas all sound good. Everyone can decide what homework you want to do, as long as somehow it is connected to dialogue.

Notice that all these lessons take place with the full class. Why do I make sure all the children are involved? Think about my philosophy. As you know, I am always trying to strengthen our community. No child is ever separated out because he or she is unready. Pulling individuals away, in fact, weakens the community. Full-class lessons ensure that everyone feels like a member and everyone has access to all discussions. Think about the message I would send to the students if I decided that some people should hear about quotation marks and others shouldn't. By itself, this decision would start to unravel the fabric of my community since it would set up a competitive, hierarchical environment where some appear to be more worthy than others of a particular piece of knowledge or a particular discussion. Furthermore, do I have the right to deny anyone equal access to all the resources and lessons in my community? I do not. So everyone hears what everyone else hears. It is only fair.

On the other hand, because we all discussed dialogue together does not necessarily mean I will require everyone in the class to use dialogue at the same time? Would you? How would this type of requirement help everyone achieve success? I give equal access to all, but that does not mean everyone will need to use the skill. That would be like saying, "Okay, since we've just read a poem, let's all take out a piece of paper and write a poem." This approach, too, would negate my philosophical and pedagogical commitment to personal choices, meaning and voice. No, so everyone need not immediately exhibit the skill and concept we just discussed. Must they know where to go when they do need to use it, though? Yes! How would they know? Remember, I taught within the context of the students' work. I "contextualized" it so the entire community knows who has already learned the concepts. Moreover, I explicitly encourage these future collaborations.

Even though the children are not "officially" assigned to use dialogue, I'm fairly sure most children will anyway. Why, do you think? Look how in this short time they became immersed in the concept of dialogue—from the very beginning when we pulled a sentence from Toni's and Henry's work until the very end when we agreed upon related homework. The children remained part of these full class discussions, and they had opportunities to talk about dialogue in teams and think about it individually during silent reading. I also made explicit connections to their future work with such questions as "Who will put dialogue or talking animals in their stories?" In this way I encouraged them to plan experiments with the concept under discussion and when this type of experimentation shows up on subsequent days, I make sure to commend it.

These have been fairly complete literacy discussions, and by now you probably appreciate how in a community where all of us see ourselves as real authors everything naturally connects. Notice the almost total absence of transition time. A couple of connective sentences move us smoothly into the next phase of work. I've been doing this for years and am still impressed by how much we get done. I love it! I even get children thinking about future work—planning a play with talking animals, I also get a kick out of how they begin to start making connections with me, even before me ("What do you think we're going to have for homework?") and laugh about it too. It is an exhilarating way to teach and learn. I wouldn't do it any other way.

But I bet you're wondering how I get it on paper and looking as though I planned it all. First of all, there's no way you can objectively plan for it all since contextualization is so personal and so complex (and paradoxically, so simple). But I definitely write lots of it down on my official planning paper.

Getting It All on Paper

Regardless of the forms I must fill out, I base all my planning on what my community needs and wants as people, authors, readers and learners. Some people might protest, "So do you even plan then at all? How can you, if you say your plan emerges from the child's work? How do you know what will emerge?"

Well, yes, I plan. Actually, I plan all the time and in a structured way. Think about it: What do all writers, readers and learners need? We all need to feel safe, accepted, successful, recognized, powerful and loved. As writers and readers we also need time to think, write, read, share and discuss such literacy conventions as dialogue, style, problems and solutions, character development, setting, and so forth. Since these concepts remain a part of my planning, and since I myself am a writer and a reader, I know the conventions and concepts I and other writers need to discuss, and I note them on plan sheets. (I am including a blank plan sheet for you to examine and also a sample plan sheet I have used.)

I use these plan sheets for weekly planning and make sure to include the major topics we will cover. Notice, though, that the topics are many and broad. Why? Again, think about our literacy community and what we do. Because the whole community engages in meaningfully personal work, and since few learners are working on identical tasks our objectives must be broad. For example, while we all work on our writing at the same time, we are all in different places in the process. Henry might be working on a first draft and concentrating on ideas, while Sheila might be working on publication and concentrating on her handwriting or illustrations. You see, then, that this type of authentic learning community makes it virtually impossible to limit children to the practice of one or two skills a week, the approach Bloom's taxonomy imposes. Would I want to mirror this narrowness in our planning? I certainly hope not. That's why I like these plan sheets. They provide a guideline, but they are broad and flexible enough for me to include emergent concepts.

Some Common Concepts Discussed Within Literacy Communities

dialogue	character change
setting	style
beginning, middle, end	suspense
problems and solutions	genre
the main idea	theme
character traits	voice
character development	character relationships
the audience	

I also write more specific plans for each day. Since I cannot predict precisely what will emerge each day, I compose these plans each morning or right after school, never far ahead of time. I usually write them in a composition book I keep on top of my desk, so I can make notes during the day. Here's how it looks:

Things To Do Today
1. Diary writing
2. Poetry ("Dreams")
3. Writers' workshop
4. Silent reading
5. Team reading
6. *Charlotte's Web*
7. Individual presentations
8. Talk about drama production
9. Review homework
10. Individual spelling tests

You'll find no skills lessons noted in these daily plans because, as you know, skills become contextualized within each activity. On the side, I might write a note to myself: "Don't forget to look for dialogue in someone's story," or "Make time for discussion about setting." I also write the vocabulary words, concepts and homework that emerge and later transfer them over to the weekly plan sheet (not really for myself, but in case someone wants it for record keeping). As we complete each activity I check it off and carry over activities to the next day if I have no time for them. Nor am I a slave to these plans. If, for example, I have no time for something and then realize it wasn't worth doing anyway, I just cross it out. I have seen teachers who seem to be on the verge of a nervous breakdown (no exaggeration) because they couldn't finish every planned activity. That's ridiculous. There's always tomorrow, and if doesn't get done tomorrow or the next day, it probably wasn't exciting to begin with. If you allow your plans to bog you down instead of becoming your true creative self, you need to think about another way to plan.

Do I just keep my "Things to Do Today" list to myself or do I share it with my community? You know. Of course, I share it with the children. In fact, we usually write this list together on the board. Sometimes I might be directive and just say,

> OK, everyone, let's write out what we're going to do today. First, diary. Well, we already did that so let's just check it off. Next, let's do individual presentations first so we can get them finished. Then we'll go on to silent reading because you are going to need a rest from listening to all the presentations.

I continue in this way until the whole list appears. Even though I am more directive here, I provide a rationale for the order of each activity so the children remain part of the decision-making process. Other days I am more flexible with the planning and just start the morning like this:

Nina:	Okay, everyone, what should we do today?
Jose:	Writing.
Amy:	*Charlotte's Web.*
Mel:	Presentations.
Don:	Reading.
Nina:	Well, I see we all want to do different things. How about this: Let's do all the things we need to do together first, then the rest of the time you can decide what you want to do. So let's practice our poetry first, then we'll do silent reading, then you can either go into writing or team reading. After about half an hour, switch over to the activity you haven't done yet. Then we'll end together by sharing and then reading *Charlotte's Web.* I'll write it on the board:

> *Things To Do Today*
> 1. Poetry (everyone)
> 2. Silent reading (everyone)
> 3. Team reading or writing (1/2 hour)
> 4. Switch (1/2 hour)
> 5. Sharing (everyone)
> 6. *Charlotte's Web*

How do you think the children react to being in on the planning? They feel valued! They feel included! This type of community planning has far-reaching effects on all areas of the classroom. The children know exactly what they will be doing and in what order. This structure, the clear expectations, and the inclusion in the planning process help children and teachers feel secure, confident and powerful. We are modeling as well how most of us plan in our everyday lives. I'm sure many of you, like me, write lists and check off each task when we complete them. Do you ever write down "objective, procedure, evaluation?" So you see, just as I strive to instruct purposefully, I try to plan this way too. It's purposeful for both the students and me, and it is fun. I absolutely love starting the day with the question, "So what do you want to do today?" It gives me a sense of freshness, a sense of freedom. I know the children feel this too, but you know my children well enough to realize that they do not choose to tease each other or throw spitballs. They love to learn and their love shows in their planning. It's so rewarding to see them during free play playing school. Yes. They play school in school. They sit as a group around the board and one child writes *Things to Do Today* and says, "So what do you want to do today?" Beautiful!

Go back to the beginning of this letter for a minute and read the quote from Goodman. Who will really be the center of your community, you and your students or some pretty sets of books and manuals by people who have absolutely no sense of who you or your students are? When you take the time to reflect on what is really right and continue to grow as a person and educator, I know you will be angered by narrow and simplistic views of teaching, learning and planning. I also know you will feel the joy and sense of accomplishment when you help yourself and your children become the living center of your literacy community.

I wish you that joy!

Nina

Nina

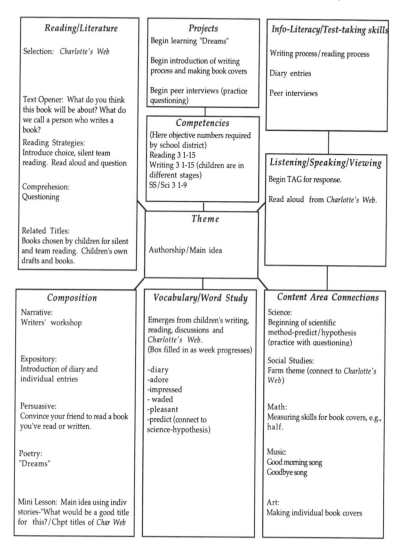

LESSON PLAN   *Date:* Sept 5/1st wk

Reading/Literature

Selection: *Charlotte's Web*

Text Opener: What do you think this book will be about? What do we call a person who writes a book?

Reading Strategies:
Introduce choice, silent team reading. Read aloud and question

Comprehesion:
Questioning

Related Titles:
Books chosen by children for silent and team reading. Children's own drafts and books.

Projects

Begin learning "Dreams"

Begin introduction of writing process and making book covers

Begin peer interviews (practice questioning)

Competencies

(Here objective numbers required by school district)
Reading 3 1-15
Writing 3 1-15 (children are in different stages)
SS/Sci 3 1-9

Theme

Authorship/Main idea

Info-Literacy/Test-taking skills

Writing process/reading process

Diary entries

Peer interviews

Listening/Speaking/Viewing

Begin TAG for response.

Read aloud from *Charlotte's Web*.

Composition

Narrative:
Writers' workshop

Expository:
Introduction of diary and individual entries

Persuasive:
Convince your friend to read a book you've read or written.

Poetry:
"Dreams"

Mini Lesson: Main idea using indiv stories-"What would be a good title for this?/Chpt titles of *Char Web*

Vocabulary/Word Study

Emerges from children's writing, reading, discussions and *Charlotte's Web*.
(Box filled in as week progresses)

-diary
-adore
-impressed
- waded
-pleasant
-predict (connect to science-hypothesis)

Content Area Connections

Science:
Beginning of scientific method-predict/hypothesis (practice with questioning)

Social Studies:
Farm theme (connect to *Charlotte's Web*)

Math:
Measuring skills for book covers, e.g., half.

Music:
Good morning song
Goodbye song

Art:
Making individual book covers

LESSON PLAN   *Date:*

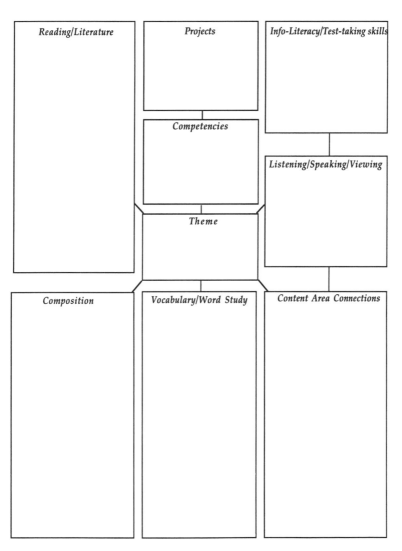

Reading/Literature

Projects

Info-Literacy/Test-taking skills

Competencies

Listening/Speaking/Viewing

Theme

Composition

Vocabulary/Word Study

Content Area Connections

LETTER #11
CLASSROOM INTERACTIONS:
RETHINKING CLASSROOM MANAGEMENT

Dear Students,

What do you think of when you hear the term "classroom management"? Does it strike fear into your heart? While I may be trying to be funny, I understand classroom management is a major concern for many of my undergraduate students and many of the beginning teachers with whom I've worked. When I discuss various ideas connected to literacy, I often hear "But what about classroom management? How do we maintain discipline? If the students aren't going to listen, how can we include writing or reading choices? Even though my undergraduate students watch me teaching third grade during the first week of school and see that I immediately establish the literacy environment and never wait until "they are able to listen," they still express their apprehensions this way:

Cindy: But how do we make them behave?

Nina: What do you mean? Aren't these children behaving?

Heidi: Yeah, but what if they don't behave?

Nina: Why do you think they are behaving now?

Dana: I don't know. I'm asking you what if they don't behave?

Nina: I like to encourage people to look at the why's of success first, just like looking at the strengths of a child before the weaknesses, so why do you think these third graders are behaving on the first day?

I know I sometimes annoy my students when I answer their questions with my own question. But as you know already, I don't believe it is my job to dish out information; it is my job to help students to develop their own voice, to be a part of constructing the knowledge they seek. So why do you think students on the first day of school successfully and positively interact as the literacy environment begins to blossom? Think about our discussions focusing on purposefulness, choice, active learning, contextualization, scaffolding and building on individual student expertise. I can hear you say, "Wait a minute, wait a minute! All I'm asking about is discipline, behavior management not all this instructional stuff. Just tell me *how we make them behave!*"

The solution requires a recognition that behavior management is part of instruction itself. As a matter of fact, it is also part of life. It is as complicated and complex as human beings are. To presume that we can manage human behavior, that we can "make" them behave, reduces children to the pets or robots that too many of us wish them to become. Is this what you wish for your students? I hope you have chosen the profession to encourage independent thinking and to promote the growth of the uniqueness within all of us.

Note the title of this chapter, "Classroom Interactions: Rethinking Classroom Management." What does this title encourage you to do? I intended that it challenge you to broaden your views on some of the terms, techniques and beliefs traditionally held in such high esteem. The change from "Management" to "Interactions" suggests an opening up of the traditionally narrow discussion of management to include the complex relationships and interactions that mark all of our lives. The one word or the other connects to the personal view we have of children. If we consider children basically evil, we will set up management techniques to quell their misbehavior and keep them on the path of righteousness. If we consider children good, we will trust them and their judgments within educational environments that support them and help develop their inherent goodness. Now let's examine this issue of management versus interactions.

The word "management" denotes a relationship where one person takes charge of another. This person applies the rules and distributes punishment and rewards. The word supports the idea that students need to be "managed" by an outsider because they are incapable of managing themselves. More specifically, students need to sit in neat, manageable rows; they need to be punished when they ignore the prescribed rules of the classroom; and of course, they earn rewards when they follow the rules. The rewards include candy or tickets or points convertible into treats or prizes.

The word "interactions" indicates a more reciprocal relationship where rules form within a respectful environment. While at least one adult (the teacher) remains in the room, this adult does not hold all the power. He or she follows the rules of the community the same way all learners do. All learners come to accept each other as complex human beings capable of personal and instructional choices. This foundation of respect and choice encourages positive interactions. The consequences and rewards within this environment revolve around feelings of pride, personal power and success.

Do you trust your children's inherent goodness? If so, what type of environment would you design to support this goodness? What type of environment might erase this goodness?

A few words serve nicely to characterize my success with classroom interactions, the same words that accompany my success with literacy instruction: love, respect, choice, responsibility, success. Indeed, one cannot really separate classroom instruction from classroom interactions (formerly classroom management). Meaningful, purposeful, contextualized instruction means positive interactions between all members of the community. Thus, when college students observe me during the first week of third grade, they are amazed to find no "behavior problems." Why not? The quick, easy answer is, "This is just a great group of kids, so positive, so cooperative." (But beware: This casual reply deflects from the examining of instructional decisions and design to the inherent nature of the children.) An answer that shows deeper thought might be, "The children feel empowered and engaged, and they have better things to do than present any "behavior problems."

Recently, I thought of a more powerful way to convey this point to my undergraduate students. Now I make sure they observe these same children with another teacher. They are shocked to see the same "little angels" turn into "devils" as they call out, push each other on line, call each other names, are always off task.

When I visit classrooms as a consultant, the classroom teacher (or principal) often tells me that "these kids are horrible. They don't listen. They never want to sit in their seats; they are always hitting each other; they never do their homework. I sit and observe and find myself amazed the children can't invent still more inappropriate behavior. I hear monotone reading aloud from material that is dry and irrelevant. I see stifling worksheets that take five minutes to finish but consume 20 minutes of deadening silence. I sometimes come close to falling asleep in these classrooms. I commend these children for not throwing their chairs at these teachers. The anger and frustration rise within me when I must sit for a half hour and listen to unconnected, boring lessons. How, I wonder, do the children control their anger and their frustration? They are continually assaulted with poor teachers, classrooms, and curricula and must sit and bear it. Most learn quickly that a "good child" sits silently and pretends to listen: They are considered the adjusted students.

The students who decide to show their anger and frustration as they hit, call out, curse and throw things are "maladjusted." These children might receive referrals to special classes because they "cannot function" in the regular classroom. These are the official weak students in need of more help. I challenge you to rethink these assumptions. Who are stronger, the students who passively accept all that is fed to them or those who express their anger over the disrespectful and oppressive situation they find themselves in? Interesting that our educational system would punish this strength. Do you see how, in fact, we might view disruptive behavior as a strength instead of a deficit?

When students in your classroom interact inappropriately, you can react to it in one of two major ways. You can blame the student with such talk as, "She can never control herself. No wonder she never gets her work done." Or you reflect on what you can do to encourage more positive behavior. How do these two options influence your interactions? Think about the first one. What happens after you blame the child? Does blame help? Does it encourage any progress? Now what happens when you step back and reflect upon the situation? At the very least, this is a more positive approach.

Blame, in fact, inhibits growth. When we blame, we place an obstacle between ourselves and our own responsibility. Teaching is responsibility. Whether the student comes to you as a second language learner, from a home you consider less than ideal or from a classroom where only negative interactions occurred, you assume responsibility for that child. But are you the only one responsible? Traditionally, we have talked about teachers as ultimately responsible, and of course in some ways we are. For example, we are responsible for setting up a caring, safe, respectful and meaningful environment. Within this environment though you can help create a community where all students, not just you, take responsibility for encouraging and holding others accountable for appropriate behavior. So, for example, when a child turns away from another child who is addressing the class, I might say to the child next to him or her "Why are you allowing Frank to talk while Emma is reading? You need to make sure you help your friends." Think about what this type of interaction encourages.

Am I giving negative attention to the child who is talking at an inappropriate time? Am I holding his or her friend accountable for community help? Does the child who is talking at an inappropriate time ultimately begin to listen?

When we begin to allow children to take care of each other in the classroom, a spirit of community emerges. Children begin to look beyond themselves to each other. They recognize that each is a valuable member of the community and each has an obligation to maintain the common rules. This type of classroom strikes a balance between recognizing individual talents and needs and strengthening a collective identity. Of course, the first thing to do is to set up a safe community where all are valued and none feels threatened by another. Sound familiar? How do we do this? Well first, we must examine strengths so that we as teachers become more accepting of our students. As we continue to work on ourselves, we can also set up our classrooms so that our children see each other in the same accepting way. Our community begins to talk about our rights and responsibilities as a community member:

Our Rights

1.	We have the right to be listened to by our teachers and friends.
2.	We have the right to receive caring from our teachers and friends.
3.	We have the right to use the things in our classroom.
4.	We have the right to call our families in cases of emergency.
5.	We have the right to be decision makers in our classroom.

Our Responsibilities

1.	We have a responsibility to encourage and be caring toward our friends and teachers.
2.	We have a responsibility to treat all things in our classroom carefully.
3.	We have a responsibility to participate in all activities and help our community to become strong and positive.
4.	We have the responsibility to help others meet their responsibilities successfully.

What I do first is eliminate all the competition I can. It's an interesting exercise to examine some of the interactions that take place naturally in our classrooms and pull them apart. Underneath well-intentioned practices I find powerfully competitive messages. Let's examine some of these practices:

Line leader

For some reason children covet the "line leader" position within the conventional classroom. To be a line leader is an honor so relished it often causes actual fights. Some might say, "That's right. That's why we need to assign line leaders. If we didn't the children would constantly fight about who's on line."

But (as usual!) let's think about this assumption. How do line leaders get assigned? Is this position on line a reward for good behavior or academic marks? If so, each child must compete for the privilege, knowing that power resides in this premium position. When teachers set up prizes to be won, active competition, hostility and even physical fights ensue. But isn't this confrontation just a natural part of the competitive spirit? Well perhaps; on the other hand teachers who foster competitiveness and reinforce it through a reward system can hardly complain about the behavior such a system so clearly breeds.

Teacher:	Wow, Henry, you really did an excellent job on the spelling test! You can be our line leader this week.
Steve:	But Ms. Burke, he's always the line leader!
Teacher:	When you decide to get an A on your spelling test, you might be able to be the line leader.
Steve:	That's not fair!

While this seems a positive situation for Henry (it really isn't, because he is being separated from the community), for the other students it is negative. Because Henry has an easier time meeting the teacher's expectations, he is chosen line leader frequently. Unfortunately, the other students rarely get this chance because most of them fall outside the narrow band of acceptance and standards.

Teacher:	On line for PE. (The students start to fight to be the line leader.) What is happening? Stop that fighting! Who did I say was the line leader?
Students:	Maria but she's absent!
Teacher:	Then Nancy, you take her place. Now all of you, stop it!

As I've said repeatedly, everyone wants to feel powerful and in control. If power in your classroom means "line leader, " naturally then the children will struggle for the position. I encourage you to rethink this common practice. Do we need to set up these competitive situations? Think about the students who never get a chance to be line leader. Is their hurt worth it?

Let's think about the whole line leader concept. Do we have line leaders in the real world, or do we just form lines in a respectful way? When we wait on line in a bank or a supermarket, we tend to patiently wait behind those in front of us. We hear no talk of line leader, and we rarely feel any pushing! Shouldn't we be helping our children with the real protocol they will practice in the community?

Meanwhile, when in later life do we ever walk in perfectly straight and silent lines? So what is the reason for all the energy teachers spend on this lining up? The same thinking allows reading to proceed through pre-planned packages called "Reading." It's a simple and easy to manage curriculum, just like straight lines in the hall.

Door holder

It amazes me to see how many efficient door holders our school systems produce. Like line leader, door holder is a coveted position. Now that I think of it, though, the same person usually fills both positions. The line leader usually seems to hold the door, and once the whole class is through the door, the holder runs up to the front of the line! Outside of our schools, the way most of us hold the door is go through it and hold it for the person behind. Why not let our children practice this common courtesy?

Helper and messenger

Certain children seem repeatedly to win the privilege of helping in the classroom. Traditionally, a helper has earned the power through compliant behavior and acceptable work. Like the line leader they have earned the feeling of power we all need. When a student becomes teacher's helper, he or she is positively recognized and placed above the other children. Here again, the message of competition is subtle but strong. It reinforces competitive behavior and ultimately disturbs and disrupts the community as a whole. While teachers think these techniques help with behavior management, and maybe in the short run they do, they still set up relationships based on competition and separation, giving some access to power and denying that access to others.

Star of the day, week or month

The student stars have usually met the academic and behavior standards of a conventional classroom, and once again, the same children are the perennial classroom stars. No doubt, these children also head the line, hold the door, and help the teacher. Some of you might be thinking, "Oh but I would do it so that everyone has a chance to be a star by the end of the year."

I know that teachers have these good intentions, but we need to go beyond good intentions and think about the messages we sent. When I deconstruct these privileges and prizes, I see subtle support for the competition that stifles and alienates our students. "Star of the Month" implies that everyone can't be a star, and the rest of us must wait to be valued. It also implies that this recognition must come from an outside source, in this case the lofty teacher. Actually, all these techniques strongly suggest this: To be a star, a helper, a door holder, a messenger, a book collector or a line leader, we must first be recognized by an outside authority who validates us with rewards. In a classroom based on competition (intentioned or unintentional) these rewards are limited and only a few can share the pleasure.

My way

My children receive no special helping positions or star status. My rules are clear and to the point, and they involve the whole community. Yes, my students walk nicely and quietly down the halls so that we don't disturb others. No one leads, no one fights for position, and we all follow these same rules:

> ### *Line Rules*
>
> 1. We stand with hands at our sides.
> 2. We stand directly behind the person in front of us.
> 3. We look straight ahead.
> 4. We walk silently so we don't disturb other classes.
> 5. We help the person in front of us follow the line rules.

Because I base my curriculum on the children's individual strengths and uniqueness, I see all students as stars. We know each other intimately since we share our personal writings, readings and thoughts. We know that Alba loves horses and that Alex loves Spiderman and that Michael loves horror stories. When children help each other as they edit written work, we learn who the experts are in various areas. If you need to work on quotation marks, go to Keisha. If you need a drawing of a dinosaur, go to Arnold. Here we are all stars because we are all special and want to share our gifts with the community.

All my children help because it is their obligation as a member of our community to be actively involved in its positive maintenance. Our community obligates us to serve others. Helping is not a special reward but a duty all share. Therefore, no matter what behavior a child might exhibit, he or she is still a part of our community and is empowered to help others. Whether Pedro has a bad day or not, he still is asked, "Please help the people at your team find the right page." A child loses no power because he or she just happens to have a bad day. Of course a child may occasionally have to pay "the consequences," but a natural consequence is not the stripping of helping behavior from the child. Indeed, when we do this we take away an activity that might help redeem the student.

Do we want to teach our children that only a few can enjoy the privilege of helping, or do we want to teach them that all are obligated to help as active community members? I contend that part of our job is to nurture cooperation and service. It is selfish of us to deprive any of our students of the joyful feeling of service to others. Remember the motto of the Knights of the Round Table: "In serving each other we become free." Do we have the right to deprive this sense of freedom to our children? We do not.

Discipline Packages: Token Economies

School districts now purchase packaged discipline methods and use them extensively. These packages provide step-by-step instructions on how to manage a classroom. Many teachers use these programs, handing out points, stickers, candy, toys and more in hopes that their students will remain obedient. These teachers, therefore, spend a lot of time and money organizing when, why, where, how and to whom points are given. At first, the teachers usually get good results. But if you'll look closely, you'll see that some children walk away with prizes and some do not.

My way

Discipline packages raise the same anger in me as the curriculum packages supposedly focused on literacy. They would have us believe that a couple of checks by a name encourages everyone to behave. We can talk endlessly about the insult to our intelligence when we are told that one program can meet the needs of all our children. But when we eliminate competitive situations, our behaviors and interactions begin to change drastically. When all children feel safe and respected by all others, positive behaviors supplant misbehavior.

I do not use material prizes or rewards to keep my students under control. Indeed, I consider token economies disrespectful, insulting and degrading. How would you like to get an M&M every time you did something right? What message does that send about you? Are you so simple, so mechanical, that a piece of candy can get you to do whatever the authorities want you to do? I hope not. I know our children are not that simple. Checks and tokens might work for a while, but that doesn't mean they are either right or ultimately effective. A smoldering anger permeates many of our classrooms (and society), kindled by the demeaning treatment so many of our students receive. Children aren't stupid. Children aren't pets. They are human beings and should be given the dignity that is their right.

I maintain an environment where a student's dignity as a human being remains intact. Students enjoy continual opportunities to control themselves and help maintain the smooth, positive operation of our community. The power, success and confidence my students feel far outweigh a sticker or a piece of candy. My children relish the personally meaningful work in which they are constantly involved. They savor their power as they help create the respectful, just and positive rules and consequences our community follows.

Classroom Rules

1.   We try our best.
2.   We listen and look when others talk.
3.   We are kind and helpful to others.
4.   We help others remember the rules.

Rewards
1.   We feel proud.
2.   We have parties and free time.
3.   We tell and write our families about our work.

Consequences
1.   We feel sad and disappointed.
2.   We lose parties and free time.
3.   We tell and write our families about our problems.

Notice the rules are broad and oriented toward individual and community growth. The consequences are clear and personal. Yes, you'll notice just a hint of tangible rewards: party and free time. What do you think my rationale is for this kind of reward? Think about what we do in real life? After a long hard week of work, what do we need? Rest and relaxation. So at the end of every school week, my children have this opportunity, too. If they choose to follow all the rules, they participate in the end-of-the-week activity. If they choose to ignore the rules, they do not participate. But that's okay. We make our choices and children should have theirs. Some choices have consequences, and then we all need to accept these consequences. No matter what choices we make, however, we are still human beings deserving of dignity.

Other Stories

A friend of mine works in a parochial school and sometimes shares her struggles and concerns about the students. For example, she tells me that the whole faculty considers the seventh and eighth graders unusually difficult, rude, unmotivated and defiant. When I asked her for a few more details, I found a couple of factors liable to account for this. First of all, like the k-6 students, they must walk in a single line silently down the hall. How do you think these older students feel about this? Imagine being forced to do something so juvenile, so babyish. Rather humiliating, don't you think?

Second, several sixth, seventh and eighth graders had been caught in a cheating situation. A teacher suggested the consequence that the guilty students stay home from the end-of-the-year trip. But as the date of the trip drew closer, the teachers suspended this consequence and all the children went. What message about discipline did these students receive?

Shanika

Let me tell you about Shanika, and let me start at the end. Shanika played the Good Witch of the North in our class production of *The Wizard of Oz*. We performed this play in front of the whole school at the end of third grade. Everyone took special notice that Shanika was the Good Witch of the North. It seemed a paradox. First, Shanika is a black girl and who ever heard of a black girl being the Good Witch of the North. A blonde-haired blue-eyed Anglo girl should have that part; it's only natural. To top it off Shanika was the terror of third grade. In the eyes of my classroom community, however, only Shanika and no one else could play this part.

I met Shanika on the first day of third grade, but her reputation preceded her—a tragic circumstance for many students—but perhaps a fortunate one for Shanika because I had requested that she be placed with me. Everyone seemed happy to comply. During our first class discussions, Shanika mimicked whatever I said, made faces behind my back, muttered words of defiance when asked to do something, and once or twice threw a chair. This type of behavior lasted about a week in our classroom and then stopped, though it continued in other settings like Spanish and P.E.

What do you think happened? Why do you think Shanika had lost her need to behave this way in our classroom? Why do you think children might behave negatively? Think about some of the issues we've spoken about at the beginning of this chapter. Traditionally, children receive an enormous amount of negative attention as their teachers apply discipline packages that advocate writing names of misbehaving children on the board, placing a check behind their name when they continue to misbehave, and finally bringing in outside sanctions after three checks (Canter and Canter, 1979). Perhaps, Shanika had become accustomed to the attention she usually received when she misbehaved.

In our class, however, she received no attention while exhibiting these behaviors. I mean none. I ignored all her outbursts. That is, I made no response at all; I neither spoke with nor looked at her. If I happened to be giving a full-class lesson at the time, I continued without any change in my body movement or voice quality. If she yelled or screamed—which at times she did—I would keep my voice at the same level. The one time she tried to hurt a classmate physically, I continued my lesson as I walked over to block the attack. The children soon sensed what I was doing, and at one point when Shanika was out of the room, I explained to the children what we had to do to help her:

> I know Shanika makes a lot of noise sometimes when we're trying to work or when you're trying to listen to me. What I'm trying to do is to give her a lot of attention when she behaves and helps, and soon she will feel happier about being in our classroom. You can help by making sure you treat her nicely so that she begins to feel happy and safe.

The children began to ignore Shanika's outbursts and modeled my positive interactions with her. No matter what kind of day she had the day before, she received a genuine smile and hug the next morning.

Nina: Good morning Shanika. I'm glad to see you today. I bet we're going to have a great day. What do you think?
Shanika: Uhmmm, yeah (smiling).
Nina: I see you're smiling! Can I give you a hug? (Even if she wasn't smiling, I would give her a hug, thus sending her the message that she was loved no matter what her behavior or mood.)

Similarly, whether Shanika had an excellent or difficult day, she got the same warm goodbye:

Nina: I'll see you tomorrow, Shanika. (I try to hug her.)
Shanika: (pulls defiantly away from embrace) Leave me alone!
Nina: Okay, Shanika. Maybe tomorrow will be a better day.

During the first weeks of school I lavished lots of attention and caring on Shanika. She received constant praise for positive interactions and work. During literacy instruction, she received the respect and acceptance all children receive in all areas of the program—that is, her work was accepted as valid contributions, she received positive and constructive responses, she had the right to give and accept help from her peers, and she shared responsibility for writing, reading and publishing what she chose. Gradually Shanika helped create the rules with the entire community. She began to follow them because she noticed they kept things running smoothly. Because all her work was personally meaningful, Shanika lost her reasons to disrupt the rhythm of the community. She got caught up in this rhythm and quickly became a part of it. When she realized she was safe and loved and powerful, she flourished. Within one week Shanika smiled, ran and danced into our community. In other words, she became our Good Witch of the North in *The Wizard of Oz*.

My friend, Beth, is a special education teacher in a resource model. Her school pulls children out of their regular classroom, and she meets them for two hours of language arts or mathematics instruction. These two journal entries describe Beth's feelings when she began taking one of my classes on writing process instruction:

10/92

"Overwhelmed" "Miserable" 12:30-2:00.
"Afternoon class falls apart (15 at one time, too much)"
"behavior deteriorates in the afternoon"
"another difficult afternoon."

11/92

"I have to go home and try to think of something to make tomorrow afternoon more enjoyable for the students and me as well."

As I began working with Beth in her classroom during the middle of the year, she confided that she had been having an extraordinarily difficult time:

Beth: Nina, I have to admit this class in the afternoon has really gotten me feeling anxious. I feel guilty about it, but I really dread when they come in.

Nina: I know that feeling. I remember the beginning of my first year of teaching. I always had a knot in my stomach in the mornings.

Beth: Yeah, that's exactly how I feel with this class. To be honest with you, I just can't stand the sight of some of them, and I feel really guilty about this. With the fourth-grade class I am much more cheerful and relaxed.

Nina: Do particular students stress you more than others?

Beth: Well, a few set the class off, but at this point I can hardly separate them out. I just have this generally negative feeling toward the whole class. What really concerns me is that I usually look forward to teaching, and I get scared I'm going to turn into one of those negative, bitter teachers.

Nina: Don't worry. One thing about you is that you are reflective and open, and these characteristics will help you find solutions to difficult problems. You know, not many teachers have the courage to step back and examine some of the negative feelings they might be having toward some students.

Beth: Well I know how positive you are with the children as they're writing, and they are really under control when you are here. But when you leave, they go back to really negative behaviors.

Nina: Yeah, the writers' workshop with TAG really helps them become positive with each other.

Beth: I know, but when I do it with them when you're not here, it doesn't work so well. They'll try and make negative comments and they'll laugh at each other's stories.

Nina: Well, how about the next time I come in I just sit within the community and watch, and then after they leave we can talk about what happened.

Beth: Okay, I really appreciate it. So then I guess I'll see you Wednesday afternoon.

As I watched Beth for the whole afternoon with this class I jotted down these notes:

Saying "hello"

Because this was a pull-out program, the students in Beth's class came from various homerooms and therefore arrived at staggered times in groups of two, three or four. As the children walked into the room, I saw them avoid eye contact with Beth or their peers. As they went to their desks, they bumped into each other or threw their bookbags on the floor or on top of their desks. Beth watched them arrive while she organized papers. Once in awhile she would look up to correct or reprimand a child.

Suggestions

As the children walk in, greet them at the door positively with a smile, hug and encouraging words: "Hi, Luis. You're here today! We missed you yesterday."

In this way, no matter what might have happened the day before, the children know that you still care about them. Even if at first this seems unnatural, push yourself to do it. Over time it will become natural and genuine. Perhaps, allow children to greet each other (you might need to model this, at first) and talk to each other until the whole community is present, then begin a community activity. Because these children come from various classrooms, it is important to help them feel safe and connected in your classroom. This positive greeting will lay the foundation for safe and positive interactions. What might also help is a favorite song or choral poetry activity that allows the children to work together immediately before they go into the more specific work at hand.

Assertive discipline

During the whole two-hour class session, Beth relied on assertive discipline techniques (Canter and Canter, 1979). If a child acted inappropriately, Beth wrote his or her name on the board as a warning. After each subsequent misbehavior, the child received a check by his or her name, and after the third check more dire consequences followed. Her options include a letter to the family, a phone call to the family, a principal's office visit, detention and suspension. Soon at least five names were on the board with various numbers of checks after them.

Suggestions

Turn assertive discipline around. Look what happens during these types of interactions. What type of behaviors receives recognition, positive or negative? Every time a child misbehaves, he or she gains an immediate reward: the name on the board. Yes, I said *reward*. We all like to see our names "up in lights." Imagine, Beth stops what she is doing and takes the time to write clearly and boldly—usually in beautiful manuscript letters —your name! And, if you act up again, your name becomes the center of attention once more. Then, if you are lucky, you get to leave the classroom and talk with an administrator. You might even miss two worksheets!

Students who need attention (and they and we all do) will do what they have to do to get it. If they get attention only when they act inappropriately, that's what they'll do. But what if they receive positive attention, too? Won't the traditional approach work then? Well, think about it. Even if it did work, within your positive community why would you want to adopt a negative way of responding? Wouldn't this threaten to undo the positive environment you've established?

But what if my school district requires me to use this program? As I suggested to Beth, turn it around. Instead of posting the names of children who are acting inappropriately, put up only the names of children who interact positively. For example,

Teacher: Wow, Sean. You are really helping Carlos. (She writes his name on the board. Then three minutes later she observes Sean.) Sean, I see you opened up your silent reading book right away! (She puts a check next to Sean's name. Then after silent reading she writes the names of children on the board who read well during silent reading, she checks the names already on the board, including Sean's.) Sean you already have three checks next to your name. Take a pass to the office so you can call your mother at work to share with her the beautiful afternoon you've been having! Congratulations!

Sean had the chance to call his mother with exciting news. Many family members react with surprise when they receive encouraging news this way. Also, you can give a congratulatory note for home, or they can write the note themselves. Thus, the children receive recognition for their positive interactions. Some might protest, "But it will take me all day to write names on the board and send letters home." I guarantee, the little time it takes is truly worth it.

Reprimands

As time went on, Beth's voice became louder and louder and conveyed higher levels of frustration:

"Sean, take that bookbag off your desk."
"Carlos, stop playing with that pencil!"
"Keep your hands off him, Luis!!"
"Sean, I said stop it, now!"

Suggestions

When Beth reprimanded her students, notice she always used their names to begin the reprimand: "Sean, take the bookbag off your desk." Once again, Sean receives attention for inappropriate behavior. He both successfully upsets his teacher, and he forces her to say his name, loud and clear. Such power, the feeling we all desire. When you reprimand a student state your sentence clearly, firmly, evenly, quickly, and without the student's name. "Take the bookbag off your desk." As you say this, continue doing what you are doing and give the child little or no eye contact. In this way, the child receives minimal negative attention.

Think carefully, as well, about the battles you choose to fight with your students. Like the definitions we adopt in our literacy program, we should be clear about what we consider appropriate behavior. If your definition of appropriate behavior is narrow, fewer children will meet your expectations. Moreover, certain children receive constant reprimanding because every little thing they do will become intolerable, and they will force you to correct every minor infraction. Overcorrection can easily start a pattern of negative interactions that becomes difficult to break. But as you will see, Beth succeeded in breaking that pattern.

Before you reprimand, ask yourself some quick questions: Is it really important in the long run that the child touched the pencil? Do I want to stop what I'm doing and interrupt the whole class? Can I ignore that behavior, pretend I didn't see it? The answers to these questions depend on the presence of praise and positive recognition in your classroom.

Praise and positive recognition

I noticed that Beth withheld positive recognition during the entire observation session. She seemed tense around the children and on the lookout for inappropriate behavior to be quelled. Unless she was reprimanding or explaining something to the class, she interacted very little.

Suggestions

Just as we eliminate chances for children to gain attention for misbehavior, we should systematically include positive interactions so as to meet their continuing need for some attention. I do this by recognizing all my students positively and in many ways. As we have seen, one way might be to write the children's names on the board or allow them to call home or dispatch notes of recognition. Actually, I do not write names on the board since I don't believe in such a mechanistic approach. I do allow children to call home and write letters if they choose. What I do consistently is provide positive recognition and invite the children to recognize to each other positively in various contexts and forms. For example, we respond to each other's work with TAG (tell what you like, ask questions, give ideas) and recognize each other with such comments as

> Carrie is ready to listen.
> Martin is looking at me.
> Sean, I see you've really gotten to work!
> Jessica, you really must love that book! You're always reading it!
> I bet you are proud of this draft, Lisa!
> You've really improved, Maggie, on your oral presentation. Congratulations!
> Laura, how do you feel about your progress today?
> Christine, are you proud of how you stayed focused during presentations?

Notice the way I provide positive recognition. It isn't exactly praise, is it? I could say, "I like the way you are listening while Luis reads, Carlos," or I could put this in another form: "Carlos, you are really listening when Luis reads!" Do you note the subtle difference? In the first example, I connect the praise to me: Carlos is pleasing me. In the second example, I still recognize the behavior, but I avoid connecting it to my pleasure. Why do you think I try to recognize the student in the second way and not the first? Do I want my students to interact appropriately just to please me, or do I want them to be positive members of the community whether I'm there or not?

You already know the answer. I always work to motivate children from within. When they feel good about themselves and what they do, they need fewer outside incentives to "keep them in line." Therefore, my belief that students have the innate desire to learn and be involved in meaningful and positive interactions and activities influences all my instructional decisions. An environment that allows these types interactions eliminates the need for manipulative and teacher-connected tactics and praise.

Token economies

I saw that Beth kept prizes in her room for those children who earned enough points for work and deportment. These points accumulated during the week, and on Friday, the children cashed in their points for trinkets and candy. During the time I observed, Beth awarded no points.

Suggestions

The token system rests on the belief that children need extrinsic motivation and awards to behave properly. Indeed, because these exchanges are so entrenched in our system, it can be hard to believe that children will interact appropriately without materialistic incentives. We need to re-examine what we do when we hand children M&Ms when they complete a worksheet. We tell them that we can expect them to do what they are told only if we give them a treat. How disrespectful an assumption! It places children on the learning level of trained pets. In some ways worse. At least our dogs avoid completing the endless number of meaningless worksheets! Over and over again, I find that a respectful environment where students do meaningful and purposeful work makes tokens unnecessary. Personally connected work is motivational in itself. Students want to do it and require no treats to get it done. Personal satisfaction and accomplishment become the rewards.

Collective accountability

While Beth interacted only when she needed to reprimand and explain, her children interacted only within a negative context—for example, "Get your hands off him, Luis!" No opportunity arose for helping behaviors or positive academic interactions.

Suggestions

Behind every set of rules in my classroom, you'll find the premise, "We help our friends follow the rules." This way I am only one person obliged to maintain the community's positive equilibrium. All members share the obligation to hold each other accountable for appropriate interactions. I reinforce this obligation often with directions like these:

> Please make sure the person next to you has what he or she needs on the desk.
> Look at the person's paper next to you and make sure the date is on the paper.
> Please make sure everyone in your team is ready to listen.
> Please make sure everyone in your team is listening.
> Henry, you need to help Javier remember what belongs on his desk now.
> Aurora, are you helping the person in front of you follow the line rules?

These directions continually reinforce the fact that all take responsibility for each other. Moreover, the children who need help remembering what is appropriate receive no attention so that negative behavior is not reinforced. The children are empowered both to help themselves and to help others. When all children feel powerful and responsible for the community, negative interactions disappear. We have too little enough time for negativity; everyone is too busy helping each other.

Strengths perspective

As Beth's journal entries and her own reflections suggest, she had become anxious about this class. She could not see beyond their negative behavior to who they really were.

Suggestions

I suggested that Beth take the time every day to force herself to name one good quality in each student. If she couldn't do it during class, she had to do it at home or sometime during the day before the children arrived. As she began to find the strengths in each child instead of weaknesses, her positive recognition and interactions became genuine. Students immediately sense when an adult is sincere. All the forced praise and recognition in the world cannot help if it is designed only to manipulate behavior.

Curriculum

Beth had begun to implement a writers' workshop as she learned about it in the class she was taking from me. She adopted the positive elements of TAG, choice and authorship, but while her children often behaved well during their workshop, Beth wasn't getting positive results consistently.

Suggestions

All curricula must connect personally and meaningfully. Why would a child want to do boring work? Would you? What do you do to avoid boring or potentially unsuccessful experiences? One way children avoid them is to act inappropriately. We must continually examine our curriculum decisions so that the work remains both consistent and interesting throughout the day. If only one segment of the day encourages choice and positive interaction—if all the other segments use such negative and mechanistic techniques such as assertive discipline—the children, too, will interact inconsistently. All our decisions must send the clear and respectful messages our students deserve.

Consistency

Beth tried hard to implement writing process but found outside pressures causing her to defer it for other more traditional requirements. Thus, while the environment in her class was often positive, it occasionally regressed to the established negative patterns.

Suggestions

We need to strive for consistency in all our interactional and curricular decisions. Positive interaction and purposeful work occasionally fail to produce perfect days in all children. But that doesn't mean we accept defeat and say, "I knew I should have kept those M&M's."

We need constantly to remember what we believe to be educationally right for children and proceed from there. The stronger our philosophy, the easier it is to prioritize classroom decisions. If we believe that children need to feel respected and empowered, we can adapt all the activities and materials that enter our classroom to complement this belief. Initially, it will take time. But the time is worth it, because gradually we will turn to what works making sure that it is also *right*! As I often tell my college students: Corporal punishment works. Whatever that child is doing immediately stops. Yelling at the top of your lungs also works. The behavior immediately stops. The question is, "Is it right?" What do you think? I think not. Respectful, positive, consistent interactions are right; we need that kind of interaction in all our classrooms.

Beth's Words

Beth implemented many of my suggestions and here is some of what she subsequently wrote:

2/11/93

Dear Nina,

Well I tried some of your suggestions, and they really worked! I made a conscious effort to praise a lot today. I tried to praise about one time every three minutes as you said, and I turned that assertive discipline around. This really helped. Scott, Manny, Kevin and Luis took home notes telling their parents how beautifully they behaved and it worked. Another thing I tried is not to use their names when reminding them what to do. I used their names only when I praised them. I had to keep reminding myself of this because I caught myself using their names to reprimand a couple of times. I also made sure to say something positive to each child before he or she left. I found this to be *very* important for *me* because it helps me resolve any anger I may have. It helps me to get over my anger so I think it may do the same for the students. All in all I had a very good day. Yes, I got angry a couple of times during the day and I did have to ask a couple of students to leave the room, but I did not feel exhausted and defeated at the end of the day. The atmosphere in the room was 100% better. In the beginning I'm sure they were shocked and some of them may have been a little frightened because only a couple of them tried to push the boundaries, but I know they felt good at the end of class because I asked them how it felt before they left and they all said they felt good. Now is the hard part: CONSISTENCY. I'm going to read those reminders I posted on the wall and maintain the following attitude "I am not taking any garbage from anyone but I will praise a lot for good behavior." I kept thinking about what you said about this situation being a great learning experience and I know you're right. If I survive this, and I *will*, I'll be much better in the end.

Thanks,
Beth

2/16/93

Dear Nina,

And another great afternoon with the 5th graders! Only two incidents could have set the whole class off, but that didn't happen. Manny, Mario and Scott ignored it when Carlos fell off his chair. This is a big step for them, especially Manny, who used to laugh loudly and make comments. I immediately praised each of them for ignoring. I made Carlos stand since it was obvious he couldn't sit. It has now been four days of incredibly improved behavior for that group.

I'm learning to take it one day at a time, but I am beginning to get really excited and happy about the change. They are trying so hard! As each day passes I feel closer to them and realize how true it is when they say that teachers learn from their students. Although they have been a difficult challenge, this group has taught me a great deal. I'm going to try something else you suggested. I'm going to let them write their parents notes telling how well they worked and behaved. This shifts control over to them. It is not me writing the notes and the emphasis is on writing to communicate.

Sincerely,
Beth

February 17, 1993

Dear Beth,

Here I sit in your room a week after we talked about discipline. You have done an excellent job using praise to turn these children around. I am amazed! I knew all the techniques we talked about are effective, but I didn't realize that they would work so quickly. Amazing! The girls are sharing now, and you can hear a pin drop. Everyone is listening, even your aide!! What did you tell her? Have you required her to be part of the reading and writing community? What a step, the boys not laughing when Carlos fell off the chair! I am so proud of Manny and Scott and Jonathan. You must be so excited and proud of yourself!

Congratulations,
Nina

3/24/93

Hi Nina,

Behaviorwise we've had our ups and downs, but overall things are definitely better. A big test came when I changed the seating arrangement. I wanted them to work in teams so I grouped the desks together. I was concerned about this since their behavior seemed to be better when they sat in rows, but I really want them to learn how to work together so I gave it a try. Everything has gone well so far. I now praise individuals and teams frequently. I know this is the key, no matter what the seating arrangement is.

Sincerely,
Beth

So what would you prefer to do in your classroom, manage behavior or encourage and facilitate respectful and caring interactions? This may be the most important decision you will make as an educator.

Keep thinking!

Nina

Nina

LETTER #12
BUT WHERE'S YOUR DESK?
RETHINKING CLASSROOM DESIGN

Hi Everyone,

Here's just a short note to tell you how I set up my classroom physically and, of course, to ask you how you plan to set up yours. Some of you may be wondering what classroom arrangement has to do with language arts. Did you ask the same thing early in my last letter about behavior interactions? You should know by now—you do know by now—that I believe language arts is connected to everything. Remember once I said that language arts is life?

Your physical design should, of course, reflect your philosophical and pedagogical beliefs. But can you predict an educator's philosophy by inspecting the classroom? Think about it. Can you automatically assume that because a teacher sets the desks up in teams he or she believes that social interactions promote learning? Remember what John Dewey said about "the thought behind the action." We need to look beyond the physical appearance and listen and watch.

I have been in classrooms (many of them) where the desks are placed in teams the but the students are forbidden to talk. A little ridiculous, don't you think? Why bother with teams if you don't want them talking? You might as well put them back in rows. Your children must talk, of course, as they help each other, respond to each other's work and enjoy each other's company. Remember, there are times to talk and times to be silent. Just make sure that purpose and meaning are the thoughts behind your decisions.

As always, a correspondence should exist between philosophy and *any* practice, and I consciously try to maintain this correspondence. So guess how I set up my desks? Yes you're right, in teams, because I believe that social relationships are the most important aspect of teaching and learning. When children walk in, they find desks for six or so teams with four or five children in a team. A quick question: Do you think these teams have names? No. Names might encourage some competition, and I want to avoid separate little communities; I want one strong community.

Where do you think the teacher's desk is, in a separate place off by itself away from the community? Well, actually it is. But do I sit in it? Definitely not! With my poor sense of direction, I probably couldn't find it. As a matter of fact, a child recently asked me where the desk was after I handed him some paperwork and asked him to "put it on my desk." The child came to me a few moments later perplexed and said, "But where's your desk?" "Wow", I thought, "what a powerful illustration of a community-oriented classroom and what a great title for a chapter!"

The teacher is an active, learning member of the classroom and, therefore, should stay out of the lonely, isolated corners. I also set up my university classroom to reinforce social interaction and usually place the desks in a circle.

Sometimes my students bring their children with them to participate in our discussions, and a five-year-old child turned and asked his mother, "But who's the teacher?" When his mother pointed me out he said, "But why isn't she teaching?" What a compliment!

What do you suppose goes up on my bulletin boards and walls to ready the room for the first day? Not much! My room stays basically bare except for the list of children's names. Why do you think I do this? Remember my philosophy? Is this just *my* community? I must wait for the children to help me design our room. For example, one of the first-day activities is to design a strip of paper. After each child finishes a strip, I staple it right on the board. In fact, it's exciting to see the room design emerge from our work. What do you think is on the walls and bulletin boards at the end of the first day? Chart paper filled with the rules we've created, the first poem we've learned, the vocabulary words that emerge from our first pieces of writing, and from the book we've begun to read aloud together. I also invite the children to bring in things they want to put on the wall—like posters, photos, or drawings.

A good friend who began teaching with me in the elementary school a few years ago walked in my room on the first day—before the children came in—and was stunned to see it so bare. After we became friends, she became a guest speaker in some of my university classrooms and typically began her talk with, "When I first met Nina I thought she was crazy! I walked into her room on the first day and there was nothing up on the walls! Nothing! Then I thought, 'I'd better find out what she's doing.' "

How will your classroom look on the first day? Will you fill it up with "your stuff" and leave no room for the children? Will you express yourself in the room and crowd other expressions? Or will you have the courage to wait to see the children's communication—to hear their voices? Do you see now the way physical design of the classroom is related to language arts?

Talk to you soon!

Nina

Nina

LETTER #13
FOR NOW, FAREWELL:
RETHINKING GETTING THE CHILDREN
READY FOR NEXT YEAR

Dear Students,

Over the years, I'm constantly asked variants of this question—from university students, workshop participants and administrators: "What will happen to these children when they get to the next grade if they aren't allowed to read, write, talk and choose, the way they did with you?"

This question strikes me as less important than, "Should what will happen next year really influence the way I educate more than what is developmentally, instructionally, emotionally and morally correct?" I am sure you know where I stand. Whether the teacher next door or across the hall prefers to force students to complete worksheets silently all day, I will not do this to prepare my children for that next grade. It would be unethical! My children might not read and write purposefully next year; I cannot deprive them of meaningful activities this year.

The question I choose to answer is, "How will your children deal with a classroom that is so different from what they are used to?" It is probably true that most of my students, at least at this point, will enter into a markedly different classroom and they will have to adapt. My children do adapt and adapt well. Let me ask you some questions to help you understand and reflect upon why these students become successful even in a traditional classroom environment.

How do these students feel about themselves?

How do these feelings influence future success, whether in the next grade or for life?

How do these students feel about themselves as writers, readers and learners?

How do these feelings influence future writing, reading and learning?

You're right, they are strong and confident about themselves as writers, readers, playwrights and performers. This strength helps them to deal with future situations. Still, I hope they get teachers like you who will appreciate their confidence and help them to become even stronger!

As I was thinking over these questions myself, I suddenly realized that my children really don't come back to visit much. I might see them in the hall or cafeteria or at dismissal. Most wave and move on. Some run up and hug me; some stop to show me a book they're reading. They seem happy, excited and independent. Within the context of human growth, they seem healthy, like growing children who become attached to and depend on their caregivers, then slowly, as trust builds, separate and explore. Initially, this exploration goes on within the sight of the caregiver, but they finally move out on their own. This is what I see in my young students as they go on to other teachers. They are confident, strong and, as I say, independent.

I confess I feel a bit hurt sometimes when I see a child in the hall I haven't seen all year and he or she doesn't run up and hug me. But this is my problem not theirs. Here's a typical brief encounter:

Nina: Eileen, Hi!
Eileen: Hi!
Nina: How's everything?
Eileen: Okay. I'm reading *Matilda* again.
Nina: Sounds great. Come and see me sometime.
Eileen: Okay. Bye.

I realize that in fact my children are healthier emotionally in these brief encounters than I am. They don't need to visit me. They feel secure, and they know they are loved, that they are special. Do they write? Yes. Do they read? Yes. In school? Maybe. On their own? Certainly.

I began thinking carefully about this concept of healthy separation and independence this past semester with my undergraduate students. I wondered who would continue to stay connected ("in touch") with me after the class ended. Even though we form a strong community during the semester, comparatively few keep in touch with me though I know many remain connected spiritually. Perhaps the ties they develop with their fellow undergraduates remain strong, as perhaps the ties of my third graders to each other remain strong as they go on to fourth grade. As I thought about this possibility, I realized that the very structure of my classroom may help explain their independence. After all my third graders saw the teacher not as the major resource but as only one of many resources. Indeed, they come to value community dependence over teacher dependence. So the fact that my former students pass on without feeling dependent is a natural consequence of the community we formed together as learners.

I found the ongoing connection between students concretely illustrated during one interaction with a previous third-grade student now in fourth grade. Elizabeth ran into my classroom with a friend before morning announcements, out of breath:

Elizabeth: Hi! Where are the encyclopedias?
Nina: In the back closet.
Elizabeth: Oh, good! (She ran with her friend to the back closet. A few minutes later, waving a piece of paper in her hands, she called goodbye.) Thanks! See you!

As you can see, Elizabeth felt comfortable coming to me for information about an impending project. No need for formalities or long greetings, she felt safe, respected and assured that she could come in when she needed resources. Sometimes, I wonder where some of my students are, and I would like them to come by and give me a hug. But I'm learning, I'm learning.

I'm learning that many students do stay connected to each other and our memories, even many years later. I recently saw one of students, Natalie, who is now in eighth grade. The first thing she told me was : "Hi! Guess what? The other night Marilyn and I were watching our *Peter Pan* video! It was hilarious.

I couldn't believe how my hair looked!"

They still talked about their drama productions in second and third grades. But of course they will remember. Even I remember their parts. Natalie was Tinkerbell and Marilyn was Wendy. How could we forget? We were involved and connected in personally meaningful, enjoyable work. You're unlikely to forget these kinds of interactions and connections no matter what happens the next year and the year after.

Here are some of our third graders on the last day of school writing their reflections. Listen to their voices, their confidence, and their excitement about the future:

Dear Diary,

Today is the last day of school. The party starts at 12:45. Today we are going to eat here in the class. Today I brought my camera, two cd's of Janet Jackson and I brought my Bugs Bunny pad. I just can't wait to be a fourth grader! The best activity here in this class was writing. I am really gonna miss the writing process and I am gonna miss coauthoring. I wanna take a picture with my camera of the whole class so I can remember everybody in this class. I think I improved on raising my hand and answering questions. I think I've improved in writing, in sharing and in publishing books. I think I've improved because I remember I used to be shy in sharing and I didn't like to sign up and share until Dr. Zaragoza put me on the list cause she said I never shared. So she asked me if I could go up and share and I said "YES." That's when I started sharing and I wasn't shy anymore. Oh yeah, that's true I improved on talking loud. Dr. Zaragoza helped me. She asked me on the play of the four habitats if I could be one of the directors so I could learn to speak loud. I said "OK," so I was a director and learned to speak loud. My favorite thing to do was writing and sharing. Bye-Bye. SR

Wow, Journal,

I can't believe today is the last day of school! The first day I came I was like a little bit scared but when I saw Jessica and Stephanie, I felt like I wasn't scared anymore. I think I have grown and you know what? I am glad we do silent reading cause you know I love it. I just loved being in this class because it is the most interesting class I have ever been in. I have grown with ability and responsibility. I just loved this class. I am really responsible and creative and have improved in fluency. See You! Bye, Journal! MR

Dear Journal,

Today is the last day of school. Now I'm going to tell you what I liked about school this year. First of all I liked my teachers because they really helped me throughout the year and my friends, too. I also liked silent reading because it helps us read and face our fears of not reading. I also like writing because it helps us be more creative and enthusiastic about coming up with more ideas. Well I have to go but I'll keep on writing. Bye. Well I'm back. You know what? I think I improved on lots of things like reading and writing. Well bye for the last time. AC

Dear Journal,

Well today is the last day of school. Gee, I didn't think it was going to be a quick year. The school year was very fun. The field trips, the parties, everything. Well I'm gonna miss my friends and teachers. I've improved in fluency which I'm proud of! I hope some of us are in the same class next year. I had never enjoyed myself in a school year like this one. Well today's the day we say Good-Bye!! LM

Dear Journal,

How are you? I'm sad because today is the last day of school. Everybody is happy but I'm not because I'm going to miss my teachers. I'm going to miss everybody but especially Lourdes my very best friend in the whole world. I am glad that I have reflected in my journal writing more and about silent reading and that I'm not that shy anymore. My favorite thing to do in this class is writing because you get to publish books and it's fun publishing books. See ya, MF

Dear Diary,

In spelling I sort of improved because we had spelling tests that were fun because we did them in a fun way. I learned how to be fluent and to always bring my homework. EE

Dear Journal,

Today is the last day of school. I'm so excited. I think I have improved on bringing my homework, getting books I like to read and not putting them down. My best is writing. I love writing and I'm going to miss my teachers. AS

Dear Journal,

I improved in silent reading and writing and I almost improved in everything. I am going to miss everybody in this class and the teachers. I am going to be ready for fourth grade and I feel great. I think everybody feels great, too. EM

Hey Journal,

Today is the last day of school. Over the third grade it's been a little tough having to have your silent reading book. Oh, don't forget homework. But it was fun. I'm going to miss my friends. Oh, I really think I improved on writing, getting ideas and journal writing. Bye journal of 95. JS

Hi Journal,

Today is the last day of school. Now we are moving to the next step in elementary with more knowledge from our teachers. They all taught me new words that I never even heard of. But now, I will never see them again because they are going to Glades Elementary. I think in this year I improved in writing because before I use to write very short journals. And I improved in reading because I never got the chance to read silently and then talk about what I read with three other people. AL

Dear Journal,

Today is the last day of school! I am very happy but I will miss my teachers. I think my favorite things I've done in this year is the theme structure and also having FIU partners because I would love being a teacher and I was like a teacher with FIU. I also think I've grown because I feel like an adult. Because now I kind of know vocabulary. And I feel like an adult. Also, I think that I have improved in a lot of things like journal writing and writing process. I will miss my friends. They were all nice. Well bye for now. JZ

Dear Journal,

Today I am in school and today is the last day of school. We are going to have a party. I have improved in raising my hand more and talking more. And how to read more in my book and write more in my writing book. What I did in the year was write and read and other things. I am going to miss my friends a lot. NM

Dear Journal,

Today is the last day of school. Yes! My feelings of leaving is that part of me wants to stay and part of me wants to leave. I've improved in things like writing, reading and other stuff. Third grade was hard but the teachers have made it easy for me. I like my teachers. They taught me to write and read and even raise my voice and do a lot of stuff. Thank you, teachers. The End. ML

Dear Journal,

Today we have a big party and today is the last day of school. I love it so much. It is awesome. I love it a lot. I feel I have learned lots of stuff. I've improved on writing and I am going to miss the teachers and I improved in journal and silent reading. Bye. JL

Dear Diary,

No! Today is the last day of school. What I like about this year is the writing. What I like of writing is the sharing part and when you make a book. I like it because I feel good and when I share stories also when I make a book it feels like if I was a real author. The best part is that you make your own stories. And, also, I like making a coauthored book. I like it because you make a story together you share together and you make [put] the story into cardboard a [cover] GL

Dear Journal,

Today I'm going to write about the school year. I learned suffixes, prefixes, FIU, how to be friends with other people, and read better, write better, talk more, books, how to be good. It was fun having you for a journal. JR

Dear Journal,

Today is the last day of school. I am glad it is the last day. But I do not want to say goodbye to my friends. My favorite thing that I did this year was silent reading and team reading. My least favorite thing was journal writing. I think I have grown by learning more words that I didn't know what they meant. I improved on getting into teams faster, getting here early and writing with fluency.

This year was fun. I also do not want to say goodbye. AA

Dear Journal,

Today is the last day of school. All the things we did here was how would you say? Um Amazing! Because I really think these educators and teachers are really what a kid would desire. First, they always helped us when we had troubles. They also made us feel secure in the inside. They also showed us how we could write stories and publish books. I'll never forget that because as Dr. Zaragoza told us just because you write one story doesn't mean you're done and I'll really remember that because I'm going to write my whole life.

Reading. I loved to read a lot but now I love to read a thousand hours, and I also like how you could do a team and talk about the wonders in your book.

Poems. Before I came into third grade I loved poems and I never knew that the classroom would have poems. I really have improved in being loud and trying to participate a lot. Since I came to this classroom I was so shy that I never liked to participate a lot. I've also improved in reading because as I said I used to love reading a lot but now I'm so excited about reading that I could never put a book down. For now, farewell. P.S. I'll never stop writing. EB

Amazing entries, don't you think? What do you hope your students say at the end of the school year?

Farewell, for now!

Nina

Nina

LETTER #14
P. S.: Some Last Thoughts

Dear Colleagues,

I've been writing to you for awhile, and I think you know me pretty well by now. Actually, anyone who observes me in the classroom or talks with me about teaching and learning knows me well because being an educator is part of who I am. When your job becomes an integral part of your life and personality , it rises above "job" to a "calling." Does your heart pound with excitement and anticipation as you step into a classroom? Are you passionate about becoming, being , and continuing to become a teacher? I am. I feel this passion whenever I am engaged in the process of teaching and learning, and it continually reminds me that I'm in the right profession.

I hope you'll reflect on a few crucial issues we've discussed here. Remember, your students resemble you more than they differ from you. We human beings all need love, acceptance, recognition, power, success and connection. When you meet these needs respectfully in your classroom, you and your children will flourish.

I hope you remember, too, that just because something works in the classroom doesn't necessarily make it right. When you educate you involve yourself in a political and moral act. You are not a mechanic fixing a car. You are not cooking. Teaching and learning happen within relationships not recipes. You are an educator involved with children who have minds and souls! Be careful! I pray you will cradle a child's spirit gently as you respectfully encourage its growth.

I wish you vision, joy and passion!

Nina

Nina

P. S.   It has been a pleasure writing to you all. Really! As you can guess, I could talk about language arts and education forever. So I really have no "final thoughts" but instead, more thoughts. I hope that we continue corresponding. I'd like to hear your thoughts. Please write soon. Here's my address:

Nina Zaragoza
Florida International University (FIU)
College of Education
University Park Campus, DM 213
Miami, Florida 33199

REFERENCES

Bloom, B. et al. (1984). *Taxonomy of Educational Objectives Handbook 1: Cognitive Domain.* New York: Longman.

Canter, L., & Canter, M. (1979). *Assertive Discipline.* Los Angeles: Canter & Associates.

Dahl, R. (1988). *Matilda.* New York: Viking Children's Books.

Dewey, J. (1933). *How We Think.* Lexington, MA: Heath.

Freire, P. (1973). *Education for Critical Consciousness.* New York: Continuum.

Freire, P. & Macedo, D. (1987). *Literacy: Reading the Word and the World.* Westport, CT: Bergin & Garvey.

Giroux, H. (1988). *Teachers As Intellectuals: Toward a Critical Pedagogy of Learning.* Westport, CT: Bergin & Garvey.

Goodman, J. (1992). *Elementary Schooling for Critical Democracy.* Albany, NY: State University of NY Press.

Grumet, M. (1988a). *Bitter Milk: Women and Teaching.* Amherst, MA: University of Massachusetts Press.

Grumet, M. (1988b). "Women and teaching: Homeless at home." in *Contemporary Curriculum Discourses* ed. W. Pinar, Scottsdale, AZ: Gorsuch Scarisbrick.

Hughes, L. (1994). *The Dreamkeeper and Other Poems.* New York: Alfred Knopf.

Kincheloe, J. (1993). *Toward a Critical Politics of Teacher Thinking: Mapping the Postmodern.* Westport, CT: Bergin & Garvey.

Kundera, M. (1984) *The Unbearable Lightness of Being.* New York: Harper & Row.

Moll, I. (1990). *Vygotsky and Education: Instructional Implications and Applications of Sociohistorical Psychology.* New York: Cambridge University Press. p. 6.

Scelsa, G. & Millang, S. (1985). *Say Hello Kidding Around.* Youngheart Records: CA.

Scelsa, G. & Millang, S. (1987). *Goodbye We All Live Together Vol. 1,* Youngheart Records: CA.

Seuss, Dr. (1958). *The Cat in the Hat.* New York: Random House.

Seuss, Dr. (1957). *How the Grinch Stole Christmas.* New York: Random House.

Simon, R. (1988). "Empowerment as a pedagogy of possibility." *Language Arts,* 64(4), 370–382.

White, E. B. (1952). *Charlotte's Web.* New York: Harper Collins.

INDEX